INTIMATELY ACQUAINTED

JEFF FIEDLER

ISBN 978-1-0980-5139-6 (paperback)
ISBN 978-1-0980-5140-2 (hardcover)
ISBN 978-1-0980-5142-6 (digital)

Christian Faith Publishing, Inc.
832 Park Avenue
Meadville, PA 16335
www.christianfaithpublishing.com

Printed in the United States of America

Psalm 139:1–6

O Lord, you have examined my heart
and know everything about me.
You know when I sit down or stand up.
You know my thoughts even when I'm far away.
You see me when I travel
and when I rest at home.
You know everything I do.
You know what I am going to say
even before I say it, Lord.
You go before me and follow me.
You place your hand of blessing on my head.
Such knowledge is too wonderful for me,
too great for me to understand!

CONTENTS

ACKNOWLEDGMENTS

I t has been a privilege and an honor to be able to share His story of how God has worked in and through my life and others around me over this era of time. Not any of it would have been possible first without Jesus Christ, my Lord and Savior. I am thankful each day for being able to walk in a relationship with Him and have Him guide me and direct me while living on this earth in preparation to live eternally someday with Jesus in heaven.

Next, I must thank my family, friends, mentors, coworkers, bosses, and educators, who have always supported me and motivated me to do whatever the Lord has brought to my path and in my direction. You have always been there to pray for me, encourage me, bring wisdom, and direct me when I needed guidance through difficult decisions and to help me be "a better me." That time you took was not wasted, and I hope you know the difference in my life you have made and may still make to this day. I hope I can give back to someone else what you have put into my life and know the impact you made or make will always be valued.

Dad, had I not grown up around a dad who loves race cars, I wouldn't have been drawn to drag racing like I am, nor had the opportunities to live out some of those dreams without you investing in me during those late night hours. Those hours consisted of laboring on my race car, welding bars, mounting brackets, and whatever else needed to prepare for that quarter mile racetrack. Thank you for always being my spiritual leader and encouraging me to be in the Word and to always make Christ priority and first place in my life. It has made a difference and I thank you, as you have showed faith and obedience and I will forever be grateful!!

Mom, thank you for always being there. Those times in life when I am faced with the "what am I going to do" situations, you always provide a caring heart and a voice in my life when at times I heard silence. I would not have been able to start my life in Amarillo, Texas, had it not been for your sacrifice to move in summer of 1998 when I got an opportunity to race with Dream Chaser Racing. I had no idea what I was doing, but the Lord did, and He was guiding me all along. Thank you for surrendering all you had to move with me and encouraging me to live out my dreams. Know I am a better person because of the difference you have made and make in my life, and I will forever be grateful for you!

Shane, although we are nine years apart, and my childhood involved getting punched with a life jacket on, roped like a calf while you practiced your roping skills, or got shot by a BB gun, you've always been the only brother that I could've ever imagined having. You always encourage me to go after everything with everything in me while keeping the Lord priority. Thank you for your encouragement and motivation if I am ever in an unfamiliar territory in life yet can always count on a familiar voice of wisdom. You have taught me how to be considerate, compassionate, and loving to other people, and those are traits I will forever be grateful for. I am thankful for your life and the difference you make in mine.

Delinda, thank you for being you. You are always there to speak wisdom about life and to lend a helping hand anytime someone is ever in need. Thank you for loving my brother the way you do and being the sister-in-law that you are and a great mom to my nephew. Often you find me humorous and funny when no one else does, so thank you for that as well. Our family would not have been complete without you a part of it, so know that I am thankful for your life and the difference you make in mine.

Reagan, even though you were not around yet or too young to remember many of these things I have shared in and through this manuscript, I hope you know you have great and incredible days ahead. You are fifteen years of age while I write this, and I hope you use some of these things I have shared to lead and guide you in the days ahead. The world will tell you, "You always have to win at everything," and the Lord says, "You don't have to win at everything." As you read through this book, you will see that I did not *win* at everything I went after...and that is okay. Strive for excellence and do your best at all the dreams you chase after while giving the Lord 100 percent of the credit and watch Him work in and through your life far above and beyond anything you will ever imagine. He can and will use your life if you let Him and know I am excited to see Him do just that with my nephew. Thankful for your life, bro!

INTRODUCTION

By default, we are born selfish, therefore not anyone is teaching us while growing up to be selfish but need to be taught the opposite, which is to share. Not once do parents state, "Now, son, you need to be selfish and not let anyone play with that car" or "Daughter, when your friends come over, I don't want you sharing your Barbies," while the child is stating, "Mine." Throughout our childhood, parents are instilling into us to share not only throughout our childhood but hoping we carry those type of traits over into our adult life, holding out hope those teachings will lead into a life of surrender.

"If we desire to fully walk with Christ, there is a cost. We may give intellectual approval and go along with His principles and do fine; however, if we are fully given over to Him and His will for our life, it will be a life that will have adversity. The Bible is clear that humans do not achieve greatness without having their sinful will broken.

If God has plans to greatly use you in the lives of others, you can expect your trials to be even greater than those of others. Why? Because like Joseph, who went through greater trials than most leaders, your calling may have such responsibility that God cannot afford to entrust it to you without ensuring your complete faithfulness to the call. He has much invested in you on behalf of others. He may want to speak through your life to a greater degree than through another. The events of your life would become the frame for the message He wants to speak through you." (Os Hillman)

D o not fear the path that God may lead you on. Embrace it, for God may bring you down a path in your life to ensure the reward of your inheritance.

> For our light and momentary troubles are achieving for us an eternal glory that far out-weighs them all. (2 Cor. 4:17)

CHAPTER 1

UPBRINGING

Developing from a child into an adolescent in Hobbs, New Mexico, I felt I was surrounded by the *perfect* family. We were the family that went to church on Sundays, Wednesdays, and anytime the doors were open. I was the kid in school growing up with both parents married and believing everyone looked at us Fiedlers as "the perfect family."

Growing up was a storybook beginning to life as I was raised how every child would desire their start. Life began by being born into a middle-income well-to-do family where I received plenty of love from a mom, dad, and brother. My dad owned his own business named Engine-Uity, Inc., which was an auto repair shop and had been in business for many years. My mom babysat for many years and would become a receptionist for an oil field service for many years. I had four loving grandparents, plenty of friends, and all the luxuries growing up that a child could ask for. At the age of five, our family relocated into a house from where my parents had originally begun, after my mom begged and pleaded for years to move to a nicer and larger home. It was in a neighborhood where I felt no one ever seemed to have problems, which seemed where the "perfect family" ought to live.

I began kindergarten the next school year at the age of five, in the fall of 1985, after moving into this house, which is where I called home for many years to come. Growing up in this house provided a neighborhood where I had my choice of many friends and provided me opportunity to learn many different personalities growing up. The one friend that stands out as my best friend was Erik. Erik and I met by living just two houses down from each other on a street named Pueblo. Erik and I both had dreams of being fireman as, after school was released daily, we would rush home to visit the local fire station, wash the garage floor out (aka the "truck hall" in fire station terms), wash our bikes (aka our "units"), listen to our police and fire scanners, and "make calls" if they were in the neighborhood nearby. In our spare time, if we weren't making calls or washing our "units," we would also issue play citations for alleys not being mowed, which we considered a fire hazard.

Growing up dreaming of becoming a firefighter, I quickly made many friends with the local fireman in Hobbs. Whether it was Fire Station No. 1, No. 2, or No. 3, I knew quite a few of them at an early age in life. I was fortunate enough during those years to take multiple pictures with trucks and even had the chance of being lifted by S-1 (Snorkel truck) onto the training tower at Central Fire Station. Logging calls on a tax ledger book, dressing in dark-blue pants and a white button-down shirt, with a scanner on my hip, and wearing a junior fire department badge is all I desired for many years.

Erik's father would later pass away unexpectedly on December 17, 1990, at an early age of thirty-eight, from a heart attack and would change my best friend's life forever. While I was still young and not fully understanding what the term eternity meant and where we ended up when we left this earth, I knew enough that we needed to acknowledge God and to ask Him into our lives to go to heaven. It was during the death of Erik's dad I wanted to make sure that my friend Erik knew that he had the Lord with him and asked my best friend if he'd like to ask Jesus into his life. It was during these days that Erik asked

Jesus into his heart and began to live each day as a young boy without a father at an early age of ten.

Going to church was something we did as a family each week, unless something else came about. My dad was the backbone of our spiritual lives and always made it known that it was crucial to attend church and read our Bibles. My dad came from a Lutheran background, and my mom came from a family who never made church a priority. I would wake up every Sunday morning (like every other child), secretly hoping we weren't going to church pretty much every Sunday. I always had the thoughts of using my Sunday mornings to play with friends, video games, enjoy family, or just ANYTHING besides go and sit through another boring sermon where this old bald guy in front of us always shouted out "AMEN" "AMEN"!

When dad took me to church, I always knew that Sunday School and big church would be involved and that I would be counting down the minutes from when the sermon started at 11:30 a.m., hoping it would end by 12:00 noon. While my dad was away or working and unable to go, my mom would take us, and I began to learn Sunday school was the only thing we would attend and go home. Being a child and not knowing, I loved not having to go to big church, which nowadays is called the service. Periodically, there would be the Sunday where we would meet for lunch as a family after church. My dad, on occasion, would work, have softball practice or games, and miss Sunday morning church for whatever reason. It was on multiple occasions where my mom and I would attend Sunday school and leave without attending the main service, which was always fine with me because it meant playtime with friends at home. At the age of nine, I prayed to receive Christ as my Savior as my dad and I had been talking about what it meant to have a relationship with Jesus and what it meant to truly give my life to Him. I remember burying my face into my bed and getting down on my knees to give my life to the Lord.

I was never heavily involved in children's activities, children's choir, or other church activities as I grew up. I didn't grow up a shy kid but not an outgoing kid so to speak. This same pattern remained through my years of youth as I would attend church but never was heavily involved in youth activities. One evening, I was sharing my "when I grow up" dreams and goals to my dad and talking about all of the things I'd like to be when I grew up, which he knew included to be a fireman and race car driver. What he didn't know was when I said, "Dad, I'd like to be a preacher when I grow up!" I remember him being overtaken by this and was shell shocked I had even said such a thing.

Tithing was taught by my dad and somewhat shown around our home but never significantly enforced. We always received those church-issued pink envelopes in the mail each quarter to seal our tithe in. Every so often, I would put a few dollars in the envelope and felt I was doing the Lord a favor by giving back to Him. I was shown to tithe by other members of the church but never continually shown by my parents, and from my experiences, you do what you've been shown, and not what they say. My mom gave when she had "leftover" money, while my dad made it known tithing came first, and bills were to be paid after the first 10 percent was given to church. My dad had the belief that if you were always faithful and obedient in tithing, life troubles would remain at a minimum. I was shown while growing up two ways to tithe and didn't feel that either one was biblical, which I'll talk more about as tithing changed my life later.

Even through all my parents' differences growing up, they got along well unless money was brought up. Money was something where they had completely different views and would eventually end up being the cause of their divorce. I never wanted to accept or believe that, one day, my parents could possibly divorce, yet the thing I feared the most eventually did happen. As I felt their separation could happen at any occasion, I always had in the back of my mind that I would never live with either one of them, if that were to happen.

My brother, Shane, which I have yet to really say a lot about, was born in January of 1971. He was eight, almost nine years older than me, so I had the life of basically an only child. I remember specifically an evening around the fifth or sixth grade when my parents had a disagreement, which I'm sure was over money. On this night, I remember hearing the word divorce for the first time. As the argument got more heated, I remember my brother comforting me and trying to make me understand that all would be okay, even by telling me, "Jeff, you know how we get in fights, and we're always okay? Well, it's the same thing and everything will be okay!" The arguing continued and eventually ended with my dad taking my brother and I in the car for a drive, explaining they would work things out and do all they could to get through the marriage. This time, they remained together, but every argument seemed a little more heated each time, where eventually, on January 13, 1996, they would split up and eventually divorce. I was scheduled to work at Subway at 11:00 a.m. on this day, which was on a Saturday. This morning started off just like any usual Saturday morning would at the Fiedler household, where my mom was up cleaning, and my dad woke up preparing to go to work until at least noon.

Knowing this was the morning my mom was moving out, I acted as though I knew nothing about the situation. I was hurting and trying to figure out how to handle this at such a young age, being sixteen at the time. My dad headed to work, and I left for work shortly after, knowing that would be the last time my parents would be together as a married couple, which I don't think had really hit me yet. I went to work fighting through tears and doing all I could to hold back the emotions I needed so strongly to share and let out. I continued strong through the shift and did everything possible to just act as though nothing was wrong and to stay strong. My dad would later come to the sandwich restaurant I worked at that afternoon, and I could tell he now knew of the situation. After moving her belongings out of the house with the help of her friend, she would make a phone call to my dad and express she had moved out and was filing for a divorce. As I continued to place meat, vegetables, and dressings on the sandwiches I was preparing for the customers clueless about my situation for their lunch, I could see the tears from my dad's eyes rolling down his cheeks in a booth from afar. July of this same year, they would have been married twenty-seven years, but as of that January day, my parents would no longer live under the same roof, and I would be added to the vastly growing divorce statistics as a child with divorced parents.

My mom moved to her parent's house, and I did what I never thought I would have to do—to choose one parent over another to live with. I was a sophomore in high school at the time and just wanted to keep everything the same as much as possible. Trying to keep everything the same was defined by me as continuing to live in the same house with my dad as I had for the past ten years. The first time walking into the house that afternoon with the remaining items which she didn't take was the strangest feeling ever. Entering a house where it echoed because many furnishings were gone, where it no longer had any acoustics, was a feeling that I'll never forget.

A life lived with both parents under the same roof was now a thing of the past, and I would continue my second semester as a sophomore with divorced parents. Though I had hoped it wouldn't change much by not having both parents by my side living in the same household, yet no matter how much I tried to defeat the struggle, it was difficult. The weeks consisted of eating dinner with my mom on certain nights and eating with my dad certain nights. Choosing to spend time with one or the other parent from week to week left a hole in my heart as I felt I was letting one or the other down. Once I decided who to spend a particular night with, I always dreaded that phone call to tell the other one, "I'm going to eat with Mom tonight" or "I'm going to eat with Dad tonight." I believe they tried their best to help me feel that whomever I chose on a certain night, the other one was okay with it, but I also felt a bit of disappointment from them each time I turned down one or the other.

Now that my dad and I were living at the house together without my mom, we ended up spending many nights together working on my 1968 Chevrolet Nova. This was a race car project that both dad and I had recently started for me to drive in the days to come. Whether we needed to spend time together or wanted to work on a race car, we spent many late nights working down at the shop welding, bending steel roll bars, making drive shaft loops, installing a seat, fuel cell, or whatever was needed to get that car on the racetrack for the first time.

CHAPTER 2

DREAM CHASER

Six months prior to my parents splitting up, on July 8, 1995, my granddad (Mom's dad) passed away from a lengthy battle of bone cancer, and would celebrate his life three days later. On July 7, the day prior to my granddad's death, I was at a friend's, looking at and checking out his new older model Ford Mustang. Riding with another friend to this particular friend's house, we were both so eager to see this new Mustang that our friend had gotten as his first car. When we went to start the Mustang (new car) to hear it run, the battery was dead, and had to jump the car off with the other friend's truck (which was his dads at the time). After jumping the battery off and getting it to start, I decided to sit in the Mustang and put the car into gear. As I tried to hold the brake with the car in gear (the truck we used to jump the Mustang off was in front of the Mustang), I ran right into the driver's side door. Not being my friend's truck but his dad's, of course, I feared the worst. We had already decided, whatever the damages were, that I would pay for it whatever the cost. A few weeks went by while waiting for the insurance company and body shop. During this time, I received a phone call that this friend's dad had been in a wreck and was okay and would lower the cost for me of the damages that I had caused with the Mustang running into the truck. I ended up paying his dad around $300, but it would have been much more costly had his dad not had the wreck. I remember sharing this with my parents, and my dad sharing with me, "See there, Jeff, the Lord took care of you!"

I was becoming of age to recognize the Lord's presence in my life, not only because of this, but at this age, I was starting to realize I have a God that wants a relationship with me and desires for me to live in a way pleasing to him and not in the ways of the world.

As the fire department passion I had for so many years diminished, my enthusiasm for drag racing was starting to escalate. I remained passionate about the fire department career but was quickly realizing that my stomach probably wasn't strong enough to handle some of the "bad calls" so to speak. I had always liked drag racing since about middle school as racing was an interest my dad and I shared as we always loved going to the races. Whether it was going to the local drag strip, the drag strip in Denver, Colorado, or just watching the national events on TV, we loved to watch and attend these types of events together.

As I stated previously, I knew the Lord was always there and always for me, but I never truly lived a life day-to-day with Christ on my heart nor desired a walk with HIM. With my dad owning Engine-Uity, Inc., he was always getting promotional videos in the mail every so often. On this particular night, he brought home a promotional video from a battery company titled *Fourth and One*, which was an inspirational video by a role model of mine who was the coach of the Washington Redskins and had a NASCAR team as well. Throughout the video, this godly role model of mine shared his love for the Lord and that through hardships, the Lord was always there and would always remain a constant throughout his life. He also expressed that each day, on his way to work, he would make a commitment to himself to have prayer time and use that time to speak to the Lord and allow the Lord to speak to him as well. After watching this video, I made a commitment to myself that every day, on the six-mile drive to school, I would pray and really begin to seek His will and, for each day of my life, to represent Him as a sign of obedience for whatever His calling might be for my life.

While watching the Winternationals on TV one afternoon during Pro Stock qualifying, the commentators announced Brad Klein, driver of the Dream Chaser Beretta from Amarillo, Texas. My brother was pursuing a music degree while attending West Texas State University in Canyon, Texas, which was around fifteen miles from Amarillo. Hearing the TV announcer say "Amarillo, Texas" immediately got my attention. As I watched copious amounts of drag racing and followed it closely, I began to realize my desire to pursue motorsports as a profession was increasing. As I prayed each day, even on my way to high school each morning, clarity began to set in. After having watched *Fourth and One* numerous times for inspiration, I was hoping my dreams and future would include a career in motorsports.

I began to put the pieces together and had the thought of going to live with my brother who was in Canyon, Texas, to finish high school and maybe even able to get my feet wet in drag racing as a part-time job as a sophomore in high school. As the gears of my mind started to turn and thinking of multiple scenarios to leave Hobbs, I became eager about possibilities as time went on. The drag racing opportunity that I hadn't even checked into yet seemed like a great opportunity, but I felt the best part of the situation would be that I would be able to live with my brother Shane and prevent being in the middle between my mom and dad in Hobbs.

The decision to move, I'm sure, sounded like a hard and unwise thing to do at the time, but I was willing to take that risk if the opportunity were to ever arise. Through much prayer, whether it was on the way to school, throughout the day, or at night before I went to bed, I began to feel the urge to write Brad Klein, Pro Stock driver with Dream Chaser Racing in Amarillo, Texas, inquiring about an entry-level part-time position.

With not much clarity nor any type of hesitation, on November 26, 1996, I wrote Brad Klein, the Pro Stock driver in Amarillo, Texas. I wrote him inquiring about the entry-level position I had previously mentioned. Brad responded on December 9 that same year, stating that at the current time, he didn't have that type of position available but to always be in touch as who knew what might happen. As I continued praying and being optimistic about where I was headed in the days to come, I received an application from Dream Chaser

Racing Engines on March 7 of 1997, stating, "Please complete and return the application." I sent the application with much enthusiasm and a bit of apprehension as it seemed a bit more real to me. I was in the state of mind that whether it happened or not, I had just turned in an application to a professional motorsports race team, and my dreams were closer than they had ever been before. Days and weeks went by without any type of response from the application I had sent back, until May 20, 1997, advising me he did receive my application and, at the present time, no such position was available, and my application would be kept on file in case something were to come up in the future.

Feeling disappointed, I did all I could to try and keep my head up while continuing to live in the current situation I was in. On April 17, 1998, I received a letter once again from Dream Chaser Racing Engines which stated,

Jeff, I will be hiring for the position the first of June that you applied for, if you might still be interested.

Upon the receipt of this letter, I was around a month from graduating high school, with no immediate set plans. I knew in the back of my mind I needed to get enrolled for the local junior college in Hobbs to attend college the next semester after high school. While knowing I needed to enroll in the junior college in Hobbs, I was putting every bit of faith I had into this career opportunity with the race team. After checking the mail on a sunny April day, a letter would change my life from that day forward.

While I was getting ready to graduate high school and not expecting anything to happen from the race team, the plans I had, which were not clear and somewhat fuzzy, were immediately overtaken by plans to head to Amarillo, Texas, and become part of an NHRA Pro Stock drag racing team.

Even though I was beyond excited to move to Amarillo and become part of an NHRA Pro Stock team, some tough days were ahead. Telling my dad I was moving was not something I was looking forward to in the least. At the time, I was still living with my dad and my stepmom and knew telling them would not be the easiest thing I had ever done. I knew breaking the news I was leaving Hobbs wouldn't be easy, but also sharing with them that I'd be moving along with my mom wouldn't make it any easier.

At the time, my mom was currently at a job where she felt stagnant and needed a change. The salary I'd be getting at Dream Chaser wasn't going to be enough for me to live on my own, so it worked where my mom was willing to move so she could help me with finances and living expenses. I'm sure, from the outside looking in, it looked as though we had this planned while graduating in May and starting at Dream Chaser Racing Engines on June 1, 1998, but I know it was exactly how the Lord had it all planned out as His timing is always perfect. As hard as it was to tell them, I knew in my heart I had to follow through with this as I had prayed and prayed for an opportunity like this and felt the Lord had orchestrated every step and knew there were great days ahead if I were to just trust Him.

I graduated on Friday, May 18, 1998, and had to be at work for my first day on the job, Monday, June 1. After telling my dad and stepmom I had made my decision to move to Amarillo, I started to pack up all of my belongings, along with my mom's apartment where she had lived since the divorce, and proceeded to head north to Amarillo, Texas, where the journey would just begin. I wasn't realizing it at the time, but I was gain-ing knowledge and wisdom of what it meant for the "Lord to Know Your Heart Better Than You Know Yourself."

I eagerly started at Dream Chaser Racing Engines on June 1, 1998, where my dream would be reached at Dream Chaser by becoming a crew member for an NHRA Pro Stock team. I thought I was on top of the world working for a professional race car team at the young age of eighteen. It was only a short time I'd have to wait to attend my first professional drag race as a crew member and anxiously find myself climbing aboard the big rig and heading to the racetrack in Denver, Colorado. I found myself standing on the starting line with drag racing legends such as Warren and Kurt Johnson, Larry Morgan, Joe Gibbs, Kenny Bernstein, John Force, and all the greats of the National Hot Rod Association (NHRA). I couldn't believe this was happening as, just a few years before this, I was only dreaming of such a job, and here I was, given the opportunity to travel between eight to ten races per year and race on a Pro Stock drag racing team. When we weren't testing or racing, we were back at the race car shop in Amarillo doing maintenance on the car, running the dynamometer (an engine stand that measures horsepower), and working on customer's engines and projects as we weren't only a race team, we were an engine shop also that built motors for other racers.

While knowing at the end of May 1998, after high school, that I was headed to Dream Chaser Racing Engines for a career, getting some type of further education and some type of degree of some sort was, without a doubt, still a priority for myself. I wanted to go after a higher education where if the racing career ever came to an end, and I needed something else to fall back on, that I had options. Even though getting a higher education didn't seem important to me from those looking from the outside, I knew in the back of my mind and had the instinct feeling that I needed and were going to get the education even though I was at my *dream job*!

I took the summer of 1998 to get acquainted with Amarillo, starting a new job, and starting a whole new chapter of my life in general. I took that next semester off, which would've been fall of 1998, but knew in spring of 1999, I would start a major at Amarillo College. I had always enjoyed blueprints, looking at house plans, laying out my *dream home* and *race car shops* during class (in our downtime, of course) in middle school at Houston Junior High in Hobbs, which is what led me to take a drafting course in high school during my senior year.

CHAPTER 3

HIGHER EDUCATION AND CAREER PATH

K nowing I needed to further my education and move forward with a degree, I realized I enjoyed both computers and drafting. I was advised to take some drafting courses by majoring in computer aided drafting (CAD) and to see how I enjoyed going in that direction. With the semester starting in mid-January and the racing season starting at the beginning of February, conflicting schedules was a concern I had, but I knew I'd figure out some way to make it all happen, and consequently, it worked out. It wasn't always easy as I found myself many nights working on AutoCAD 2000 Student Version back at the hotel during racing weekends, but I always seemed to have projects completed by the date they were due. During the week, while working at the race car shop in Amarillo, I left Dream Chaser many nights. changing from work clothes to school clothes, headed to a community college to take evening drafting classes. I continued this trend of working and attending college for the next five years while working full time, which, at the race car shop, meant sixty to sixty-five hours per week.

I had almost two and a half great years at Dream Chaser Racing Engines, where I had met many people in the racing community, received a wealth of experience on how to work on race cars, how a machine shop was operated, and was taught that working hard was the only way to be "successful" in this dog-eat-dog world we all encounter each and every day. I was able to live a dream of working on a Pro Stock drag racing team from June of 1998 until the end of September of 2000, which was when I started to feel I should focus more on my education and my drafting career. I knew the field in drafting, or some other type of career, was needed to make a living as I knew deep down that Dream Chaser Racing wouldn't pay much more than I was already taking home, which was around $378 dollars every other week. Some situations happened at Dream Chaser which I felt weren't in line with my beliefs and had been feeling frustrated awhile before; therefore, knew it was time to move on. Even though leaving was hard, I knew I needed to pursue a career in drafting.

As I searched for job opportunities, I became further excited about moving in that direction. I was not sure where to find drafting jobs, but thought the yellow pages in the phone book would be a great start. Well, lo and behold, I came across a place that copied and printed blueprints and believed this would be a great direction to head in. I called and inquired about an entry-level job opportunity, and before I knew it, I was heading there for a job interview and walked out of the building an employee of this blueprint company, which was Monday, October 2, 2000. I happily worked for this company for a short but great six months. Duties at the blueprint company included running copies, scanning, and printing blueprints for residential and commercial projects for various builders, architects, and design firms.

While contently working there, I happened to run across a surveying firm that was hiring for a drafting and field surveying position. Knowing the blueprint company was just a step into my career, I inquired about the position I happened to see online and was given the opportunity at an interview. As the blueprinting company was a step in the right direction for my career, I felt a land surveying company was the next place, which was more of a career opportunity that offered 401(k), insurance, benefits, and paid holidays. I became employed with this surveying firm in March 2001. This would be a place of employment where I sometimes felt stressed, but looking back, I now appreciate some of the tougher days while employed there. I was taught at this firm how to draft title improvement surveys, subdivision plats, surveying duties, which included locating corners, setting corners and benchmarks, and various surveying and drafting duties. While working at the surveying firm and attending a community college, being in my early twenties, I felt that my career was headed in the right direction. I thought, *I'm going to school and working for a successful surveying/engineering firm, and things are going pretty well!* And they were from March 2001 until September 2003 and then I felt it was time for a change.

While still employed at the surveying firm, in the summer of 2003, I started to feel a tug on my heart to coach T-ball or some type of sport through an organization where I would be serving and making an impact on someone's life. If you've never watched the movie *Hardball,* it's a movie about a guy that becomes a coach for a group of kids that are playing street ball, and the team ends up winning the Little League Baseball Championship. The thing that stood out to me the most about the movie is the coach develops a friendship with each of his players and truly becomes a "family like" team. *Hardball* is the movie that inspired me to want that same thing, which was to help them learn and play the game of baseball and, mostly, develop a friendship with the kids and their parents, act as their mentor, and become involved in an organization where I had visions of them investing into students' lives besides playing a game. I inquired and investigated into something that would allow this and came across an organization that offered this. I started coaching T-ball in summer of 2003, which was a great first year of coaching, and I knew this would be something I would want to do for many a year to come.

During this first season of T-ball (2003), I met Eddie, Robin, Lauren, and Josh, which was an incredible family that would end up making a huge impact on my life through the years to come. We had a great first year, and at the end of the season, all of us knew we would continue the next year. The next year (2004) was when James R., which I will talk about more in-depth later on, would become one of the coaches and ended up coaching alongside of me during the next several years while building relationships and friendships with the parents at the same time. I would meet Kevin and Nicole, whose son is Seth, as we, too, would also become close through the years while Seth played on teams all through the many seasons James R. and I coached, until the end of 2009.

Taking drafting classes during the evening while working at the surveying firm during the day, I was feeling drawn toward a liking of residential drafting and design. Many knew that I was ready for a change from the surveying world and was looking for a change in jobs. My mom had been looking through the paper, and in the classified section was where she found a job posting by a company called The Drawing Board, which was a residential design firm looking for an architectural drafting position. I contacted The Drawing Board about bringing a resume and the possibility of getting an interview. After looking over my resume and reviewing the candidates, I received a call a few days later and was told management thought I would be a good fit for the position they were looking to fill.

Without knowing I would be starting a career, in late September of 2003, I started working at The Drawing Board

(TDB), feeling inexperienced in residential and commercial drafting. While feeling green in those areas of design, I had knowledge of the AutoCAD software while working toward an associate degree at the community college. Prior to being employed at TDB, I was fortunate enough to work for the surveying firm I spoke of earlier, therefore, also gave me a vast amount of the AutoCAD software experience needed for the next step in my career. The days would start to fly by while being employed at TDB. Weeks would turn into months, and months would turn into years. The more I learned at The Drawing Board, I started to quickly realize I truly enjoyed what I was doing and would start to build work relationships and friendships over the years.

The Drawing Board was owned by Jack and Sandie, run by Jack each day, while Sandie was a math teacher for an independent school district at a high school. Timothy was the lead draftsman at TDB and was reaching close to ten years with this firm when I started in 2003. Jack and Timothy were more the designers of the projects, while I was starting to learn how to finish the projects as far as the electrical, elevations, roof, site, and foundation plans. It seemed as if I would never get a grasp on this career as each project differed. Every day left me feeling as though I would never grasp this occupation, but with continued determination, I continued to learn more and was starting to take on projects and finish them myself without assistance.

I grew to have more of a liking for the business side of things rather than the design side. Jack and Timothy liked the design side and did not care much for the business side as far as invoicing, making appointments, payroll, and day-to-day office duties. Sandie (Jack's wife) approached me about doing daily office duties which included invoicing, payroll, and making new folders for jobs. By about the fourth or fifth year of employment at TDB, I became heavily involved with day-to-day office duties including invoicing, creating job folders, and getting people in place to get a website designed for the company. The longer I was employed there, the more I realized that this job was for me. I started to build relationships and have good friendships with the builders that used TDB for their plans. I had possession of a key and was able to come and go as I needed. I got to where I would work until 1:30 a.m. or 2:00 a.m. the next morning on occasion.

I found myself working harder for this company more so than I ever had done anywhere else, and the main reason being, because they trusted me and knew I would always get the tasks done that needed to be completed. While working as hard I did for this company, there were many that thought I was being taken advantage of by the hours I was working and using my personal vehicle for job measurements and errands, without getting reimbursed for my time and resources. While it bothered me a little, it bothered me more that others were so concerned about getting compensated for every little thing and not able to see what I did have. I was working for a Christian family that loved the Lord and had a company that was investing and allowing me to get whatever experience I wanted. I also had a company that was willing to build long-lasting friendships through this company which, for some reason, I knew would work to my advantage someday as the experience I was getting would be beneficial.

> Work willingly at whatever you do, as though
> you were working for the Lord rather than
> for people. Remember that the Lord will give

you an inheritance as your reward, and that
the Master you are serving is Christ. (Col.
3:23–24)

Having now graduated from a community college with an associate degree in May 2004, I knew I needed to further my education level to at least a bachelor's degree. I knew that no college or university around offered any type of architectural degree, therefore, I needed to have a bachelor's degree of some type. Knowing I had always wanted my own business, I, therefore, felt getting a bachelor's degree in business with an emphasis in management would be a good quality to have. I started to attend a four-year university in the fall semester of 2004. While working full time, I balanced work and school together and graduated with a bachelor's in business in December of 2009.

CHAPTER 4

FINANCIAL SETBACK

It was never my intention to go into debt, which I'm sure is what everyone says when they get their first credit card. A credit card by a bank was my first credit card to possess in 1998 and carried a high interest rate. I probably wasn't in the best position financially to be moving to another state when I had the opportunity to leave Hobbs and move to Amarillo. I had some finances set aside for a few moving expenses, but when it came right down to it, I believe around $800 was what I had in the bank at the time of the move to Amarillo. Throughout the time I was employed by Dream Chaser, I was taking home $368 dollars every other week which, as you realize, isn't much money. Looking back now, I realized that my mom moving along with me was the only way I would've been able to move. Things were tight financially even though we lived in an apartment. After paying rent, bills, food, gas, living, expenses, and whatever else that needed to be paid, there wasn't much left over after each payday. This was one concern of mine of enrolling at a college, having the thought of how I was going to be able to afford classes, tuition, and books at this community college. This was where the credit card would come in. Making what I made wouldn't allow me to pay for the expenses required to pay for a higher education. The problem with a credit card is that not only was I starting to put college expenses on it but was justifying many other expenses as far as clothing, food, and whatever else I wanted without having to pay for it at the time of purchase.

My intention throughout getting this card was to charge things and then, each month, to pay the statement off in full, but as the balance became higher and higher, it was beginning to be unattainable as the balances grew, especially with the interest rate as high as it was. I went on like this for many years through-out the two-year college days until 2004, which was when I would be able to close the chapter at this community college and begin a higher education at four-year university in 2005. I knew that was going to be a task financially, and I would not be able to attend without some type of financial assistance. It was then I realized student loans would have to become my financial source to be able to pay for tuition each semester at this university as tuition and books were running between $3200 and $4000 each semester, depending on the number of hours I would enroll in, ranging anywhere from nine to twelve hours a semester. By the time I graduated with a bachelor's, I would find myself owing close to $40,000 in student loans. It was July 16, 2010, that I started having to repay those back at the amount of $294.93. In May of 2019, I refinanced my student loans, which upped my payments, but will cut around twenty years off the total.

In July of 2013, I decided that getting a personal loan would assist me to get some things paid for quicker and cheaper than continuing to use credit cards, which I'd hoped to get where I had only one payment instead of multiple credit card payments. This was a $25,000 loan and was paid until the fifth of September 2017, and this was paid in full on this date. Those payments for the personal loan were $583.15, due on the fifteenth day of each month.

When you are willing to put yourself so far out on the limb, when you know God has spoken, that if God doesn't come through, you're going to utterly fail. That is what it means to trust God. (Unknown)

I did everything I could to lower the debt-to-income ratio that I suddenly felt burdened with. Between student loans, credit card debt, and now a personal loan, I owed upward anywhere from $75,000–$80,000. The justification for not tithing was that I couldn't afford to tithe because of living from payday to payday and felt I didn't have the resources to tithe. The entire time, while telling myself, "I couldn't tithe," all while not realizing, "How could I afford not to tithe?" Even though the debt was high and seemed to rise, as it seemed as though something else would come up, I felt I could pay bills and lower debt with tithing money. It did seem that debt was lowering, but it would lower one month and increase the next. It seemed like a financial roller coaster as I knew I was continuing to fight with the Lord with my finances, knowing even though deep in debt, tithing needed to be a priority.

CHAPTER 5

CHRISTIAN FELLOWSHIP

Church hadn't been much of a priority since moving to Amarillo in June of 1998. I knew that it was something that needed to happen, but I had not at all made it a priority, although I knew in my heart that I was lacking something each Sunday that rolled by from 1998–2003. A local Baptist church was where it all began for the start of my confidence for who I was in the Lord and where I found my identity in the Lord. I started to attend this church in 2003 and became heavily involved in orchestra and, more importantly, had an accountability group like I never had before. There were about twenty solid godly people I could count on and knew would be there at any given moment in a time of need—for accountability or just a time to hang out with a godly inner circle. One of these people in this group was James R., who assisted me in coaching kids and adolescents starting in 2004. I always had a vision of what an inner circle looked like but had never experienced it until the end of 2003 through 2009.

Getting introduced into this accountability group, I was advised that each Wednesday night, I would need to go to a house on Bowie Street, and it was there that I would meet The Biggers family. This was a family like I had never met before. At any given time, there were twenty to thirty hungry (both physically and spiritually) college students at this house each week. After this family had worked a full day, they would come home to their residence and allow it to be like our own home for a couple of hours. It was in the kitchen and in the living room of this residence where these college students met to have fellowship and a time of worship. Looking back and not grasping how much of a difference their sacrifice made at the time but now realizing and knowing that it was there on Bowie Street, in that house, that the Lord shaped and molded me and started a work in me like I'd never experienced. Along with weekly Bible Studies, often led by David our college pastor, and meals, we had fellowships, road trips, fun, and I grew spiritually more so than I ever imagined. Just after a few short years after moving to Amarillo, the Lord provided like He always had and supplied a support group for a group of college students that needed this, more so than the group and I ever realized. Many of us still keep in touch today and not ever doubt that those years were the years that taught many of us how to love, share, surrender, give, and to not overlook someone or, in this case, a college group that needed life direction.

I was living with my mom as I started to attend this local church, but as time went on, I got to know a guy named Joe, who also visited this church about the same time as I did and had just recently moved to Amarillo to attend the local law enforcement academy. Joe and I had become good friends, and through this college group, we decided it would be fun to be roommates in October of 2004. While Joe and I had planned on being college roommates, thinking it would last six months to a year, six months turned into a year, and a year turned into two, and two turned into five. I lived with Joe for five years, even moving into a house with him as he purchased a house so he would have one for when the right mate came along, that he would have a house for his wife someday (which Joe stated several times, but he definitely wasn't in any hurry).

While Joe dated off and on, we would have discussions nightly about when was the right time to be married, who was the right person to date to marry, and who we thought would be good to date as far as marriage material. Joe was way more interested in this dating marriage talk than I was but I thought, well it's probably not a bad thing to have a Christian brother to share about dating and marriage as he liked to talk about such things, so I seemed to always engage in conversation about those topics. Neither one of us were actively pursuing anyone to date, but we always seemed to have the college group from this Baptist church over, first at the apartment and then after the house purchase, which didn't change a thing except we had more college students over since we had more square footage to hold more friends.

I decided to partake in a mission trip to Arlington, Texas, in 2005. It was a mission trip to focus on cleaning up some apartments that had been run-down and were needing a facelift. The church I was attending had taken a group there to assist with the project. It was on the way there, where I would meet a girl named Elizabeth. Elizabeth was the only one from her church to go on this trip as she piggybacked with our church to partake in this mission trip. Elizabeth and I hit it off quickly by talking and just getting to know each other better on the way there and on the way back. Elizabeth and I had quickly become good friends and started to see each other more, and before I knew it, we were spending quite a lot of time together. I knew, or thought I knew, what I needed and wanted in someone to date, and I believed this just so happened to be the "perfect" one.

Up to this point, I had never dated anyone but felt the Lord had put something in me to know exactly what I wanted, if and when that ever happened. It so happened the Arlington, Texas, trip would change my life for the next three or so years, all along I was feeling this was the one. I knew what the Lord had laid on my heart in what to look for in the opposite sex, which entailed someone that was, number one, a believer. I desired to be with someone who was not only a believer but for her to be passionate for the Lord. I always had it on my heart for this person to lead worship in some form or fashion, and Elizabeth played drums and guitar and led youth worship at her church. I longed for someone to pray with and just to share what the Lord was doing in each of our lives, day in and day out. Not really anything spectacular or magical, I just felt

I needed someone to share the day-to-day of "this is what God did today" or "this is what I expect the Lord to do tomorrow."

I've always yearned for someone that had not only self-confidence but self-confidence that was Christ given and secure in who they were. The more I got to know Elizabeth, the more I realized she had every one of these qualities, and more so. She was raised in Taiwan and raised in a missionary-minded family. Elizabeth was a leader which led her to become a Baptist Student Ministries (BSM) leader at the school she was attending. Elizabeth was passionate about the Lord, how He led her each day. As weeks went by, I felt she was the one to pursue and knew without a doubt God revealed every trait and quality I had vision of and felt the Lord had laid her on my heart for a soul mate. A lot of the time throughout 2006, Elizabeth was going on random mission trips from Taiwan, Hong Kong, and whatever city she was called to next. It was hard to not be around her, but I knew she was doing what the Lord was leading her to do, which was the only thing that brought me peace while being away from her.

As time went by, and weeks became months, I was starting to feel there might possibly be something there between us. At this point, I wanted a relationship with her more so than any-thing else. She seemed to be everything I had ever dreamed of a girl being, and then some. For three to three-and-a-half years, I wanted to spend any and all my free time with her to make it known this was "the one." Well the day(s) came that she started to see other guys, and I started to figure out with some conver-sations we had that maybe the Lord didn't have a plan for us after all. After allowing myself to fall without holding back for over three years, I was *crushed*, to say the least.

Some of the people closest to me and around me shared, "Jeff, we just don't see what you see in her" and conversations like, "You have deserted the rest of your friends only to be with her." I didn't want any part of these conversations to be true, but as time went on, I started to realize what I had done to my sup-port group and my friends. I had gone from feeling as though this might be the one and threw myself out there for over three years and then it abruptly came to an end, which I couldn't and didn't want to understand. Elizabeth was everything imaginable the Lord had shown me that I wanted, yet I felt He was taking her away, therefore, we no longer spent time together.

It took a while to realize that the timing for me to be in a relationship and looking into marriage wasn't then. This is something that only the Lord knows—what I need and what my heart desires. I've tried and will continue to rely on the Lord for Him to bring what I need and desire because "God knows your heart better than you know yourself." As much as I felt Elizabeth was the one, God knew there was more He had planned for my life. As you read on, you'll see the things I would not have gotten to do had I been in a serious relationship or married!

CHAPTER 6

OUR PLANS CHANGE BUT NOT GOD'S PURPOSE

As hard as it is to accept, when things don't work out, don't force those things. There is so much the Lord has in store for your life, therefore, when there seems to be roadblocks, don't continue to press through the roadblock and attempt to get through. I believe when things don't work out, He had his hand of protection on your life and was possibly keeping you from circumstances that might have harmed you or where He had something so much greater for you, *but only in His timing*! It is difficult to understand while you're going through it, but realize there are people that God has put in your life to help steer and direct your life in and through their experiences. God doesn't, has never, and never will make a mistake, so listen to people who are *intimately acquainted* with Him so they can speak wisdom and life into you. Your Christ-centered friends care about you, and whether we realize it or not, they can sense things you and I cannot, which I'll experience a bit later through a career change.

I attempt to always picture God as being a GPS, with God looking down on my life, therefore, I refer to it as the "God Positioning System." I've tried to view it as though when we are looking for a location to be directed by a GPS, the same way we are relying on a voice from a satellite to direct us, that when we're in tune with God throughout our lives, it's like a GPS. When we're on track and follow the path, we reach our destination and feel a sense of completion. It's the same but with God directing our path, allowing Him to guide us. Prayer life and seeking Him is a way for us to know the direction our lives are meant to head in, so be in constant prayer, and each day, act as though God is your GPS. Don't ignore that direction as He desires our souls to follow His lead and know our lives should follow the small quiet voice heard in your heart.

Early 2008 was when I would learn that my friend Joe and Melody would become engaged, and May of 2010 would be the wedding day. This was great for Joe but left an unknown living situation for me. I knew this day was coming and knew I probably couldn't afford an apartment alone while my only income was The Drawing Board. I knew Joe was getting married in the days ahead, and I hadn't thought too much about where I was headed for living circumstances but knew something would come along to allow for me to live on my own.

The beginning of the 2009 youth softball season was when I would meet two brothers named James K. and Josh. We started practicing usually toward the end of school in May, and season would start in middle June and run into middle of July. It had only been our second or third practice when a couple of kids came up to me and said, "Hey, my brother and I would like to play this season with your team if you have any spots available." My initial response was "We're actually pretty full right now, but I'll let you know if we have any spots open up." We did have a couple of players quit, which opened a couple of positions for these two brothers named James K. and Josh. As I got to know more about these two, I began to care about them and connected with them more so than if they were my own kids. There was just something about them that the Lord had laid on my heart to reach out to and for me to go out of my comfort zone to care for them like I'd never done for anyone else. The more I got to know James K. and Josh, I learned that Seth (who was on my team from 2004) was the one that invited them to the softball field that day to practice. I got to know James K. and Josh more each practice and would eventually have a caring and love for them that only the Lord could have given me.

Midway into the softball season, I had asked Lindsey (their sister), who was James K. and Josh's legal guardian, if another friend of mine, which was James R., and me could take them to lunch to get to know them better before playing on the team. I remember this day specifically because, while inquiring about lunch to Lindsey, my voice was trembling even if it was only to ask if we could take them to lunch.

Lindsey replied, "Jeff, are you okay?" as she could hear my words shake.

I'm not sure to this day why my voice quivered as it did as the only thing that comes to mind is the Lord was going to do such a work in and through James K. and Josh. He allowed me to have a glimpse of His plan for them, which overwhelmed me and excited me all at the same time without having an indication of what He had planned for the incredible days ahead!

It was at lunch (which was at the local Cheddars) where I learned that James K. and Josh's mother had passed away suddenly on July 10, 2008. These boys grew up without their father in their lives and, having recently lost their mother, it would be a hard way to grow up. I felt they would face many challenges to come in the days ahead while not having their father or mother in their lives. This tragedy would be tough for anyone to endure, but with James K. being thirteen and Josh, eleven, broke my heart for them.

After lunch on that Saturday, June 6, 2009, we became like family. We continued to play several softball games through this 2009 season. James K. started out as pitcher, and Josh would play third base and outfield. As I became closer to them and as the summer got closer, I mentioned something about church to them. We had the normal "I go to church on occasion" or "we go here and there" conversation, but nothing too in-depth. While I was still awaiting an answer from a Baptist church on a youth minister position, I was hoping James K. and Josh would become part of the youth group that I wasn't part of yet, but I didn't want to rush anything. As the summer went forward, we started hanging out more, playing video games, taking trips, and eating out. They truly became like a second family to me and became a *sacred concern* as I was always eager to spend time with them and be a positive influence in and through their lives any way I could.

CHAPTER 7

THE SIGN

E ddie (whom I met back in 2003 through T-ball) was always involved in ministry of some type, whether it was PTA, youth camp, youth groups, feeding high school kids for lunch, and would become a pastor of a couple of different churches. Over the years, I think Eddie could see my heart for these softball kids and brought up the topic of "Would you ever want to help out in youth ministry at our church?" While I didn't feel led to serve at the church where Eddie was, I did start to feel a tug on my heart to be involved with some type of ministry. It was literally only a few weeks later, after having that discussion with Eddie, where I would drive down Bell Street and see a church marquee sign, "Part-Time Youth Minister Needed." I immediately inquired about the position and applied. At the time I applied for the position was somewhere around late February or early March of 2009, and I received the call late summer that my first Sunday would be August 9, 2009. I was ecstatic that

I would get to fulfill my longing to minister to youth and be on staff at a church, which felt like my childhood desire to be a preacher would be fulfilled.

The long-awaited answer (roughly nine months) finally came from this church where I was the applicant chosen as the new youth minister. I couldn't even express the excitement after receiving the news that I'd be the new youth minister at a church as I knew the Lord was going to do some mighty and incredible things, and He did, way beyond my imagination. I went to this church each week thrilled to see what it was that the Lord was going to do next. The months of August and September were going great as we had more youth attending each week on Wednesday nights and Sundays, and we knew the up and coming Revival promised to be a powerful time. This church, where I was now the youth pastor, had a Revival every other year, and it just so happened that this year, 2009, was the year for it to return.

The Revival started on a Sunday morning, October 11, and ran all the way through that following Wednesday, which had a "youth" emphasis attached to it. That Wednesday, we had roughly fifteen to twenty youths that night. The speaker that night was an evangelical speaker named Paul, who also led the Revival in its entirety, but only God knew what He was going to do on this night, October 14, 2009. We had eaten pizza, sang songs, and listened to a message, which was when three lives were changed for eternity, and two of them being James K. and Josh. While the music played and the invitation started, Josh was quick to get up, fighting to get through everyone in the aisle to accept Christ in his life while weeping to the point of being overwhelmed. James K. would quickly follow and then another, to surrender their life to the Lord.

It was a time when, in just a few short months, three youths would give their lives to the Lord, and God was quickly doing a work we couldn't even fathom. The night would be followed by an e-mail by the Baptist church pastor:

> I believe we just witnessed the most awe-some demonstration of God's power being displayed that I have seen since I left the Philippines 8 years ago! I truly have no words to describe it except GLORY!!!!! I believe God is doing something so amazing that we can't

even begin to fathom the extent of what He
is doing in our midst.

This night was beyond anything we could've ever imagined, and
the fact that two of my youth softball kids were *saved* while being their
youth pastor for roughly eight weeks was incredible to me. Knowing
James K. and Josh would spend eternity with me brought me a peace
and anticipation for what God was going to do in and through them
beyond anything I've ever experienced. In the days ahead, I would
see James K. and Josh's relationship with the Lord grow stronger and
stronger through prayer, worship, church, and they truly became two
completely changed individuals. There were times I would pick Josh
up at school in middle school, and he would tell me, "I gave a Bible
to someone today" or "I talked about Christ to a lost person today"
and many more examples how Josh was continually planting seeds.
Whether it was being on a softball field, at church, See You at The
Pole, or wherever it was, Josh was making a difference.

One of James K's biggest struggles was cursing, and now being
saved and a born-again believer, James K. was convicted about his
language, which immediately was cleaned up. James changing his
language so suddenly was a shock to people around him and made

them question what was different. Therefore, I believe strongly it is so important to truly walk the walk because lives are affected each day by how you live your life as people are watching and listening to you, whether you know it or not. After just a short time of James K. and Josh becoming saved, they wanted to follow in believer's baptism and reveal to the church that they were now followers of Christ and wanted to make that publicly known. Sunday, October 25, 2009 would be my first baptisms, and the first two I'd ever taken part in were Josh and James K.,

Psalm 139:7–9

I can never escape from your Spirit!
I can never get away from your presence!
If I go up to heaven, you are there;
if I go down to the grave, you are there.
If I ride the wings of the morning,
if I dwell by the farthest oceans,

CHAPTER 8

SACRED CONCERN

As time went on, with James K. and Josh having become more active in church, while still playing softball and starting to become more active and involved in school activities such as basketball, football, art, and pole vaulting, I found myself becoming extremely close to these two brothers. I couldn't figure out why my heart was not hurt for them, yet I had compassion for them after losing a mom a year ago, while not ever having their biological father in their lives. It was not a situation where I treated them differently than the rest of the youth kids, but on the other hand, I had tendency to expect more from James K. and Josh as if they had become my own two kids. We got where every Wednesday night after youth service, we ate dinner before taking them home. At this point and time, I was struggling financially, which I will talk about later, but nothing kept me from providing for James K. and Josh to grow our relationship between us and for me to get to know them better. Not only were we eating out each Wednesday after church but also each Sunday at lunch and Sunday night. The more we got to know each other better, the more I found myself doing more. Josh and I ended up taking trips together to mountain bike, getting new school clothes, or whatever I could do to provide for them and make quality of life greater for them as much as I could.

> In his kindness God called you to share in his eternal glory by means of Christ Jesus. So after you have suffered a little while, he will restore, support, and strengthen you, and he will place you on a firm foundation. (1 Pet. 5:10)

I was not in any healthy form or fashion financially, but I was able to do all I did for James K. and Josh, and many a time, I found myself charging meals, clothes, school supplies, and trips to a credit card. But for some reason, that never bothered me as I felt deep in my heart, *It will all work out one day, and it will be okay.* I found that the more I provided for them, brought them happiness also gave me even more happiness. I couldn't figure out how going more and more into debt would satisfy, but it did, and it brought me joy to provide any and all I could for them. No one else had any knowledge of what I did for James K. and Josh except them. Though them (or anyone else) not knowing I was moving further in debt providing for them did not even bother me. I felt if I had told anyone, they would have felt differently and probably expressed that I shouldn't be increasing debt providing for someone that wasn't even related to me.

Not I, myself, could understand why I had such a longing to provide anything and everything I could for them, but it was something I felt that could not be ignored, and I believed wholeheartedly that it was a calling from the Lord to do so. I went many years (2009–2017) providing for two brothers that weren't even kin to me, but somehow, the Lord provided ways to bless them (even through a credit card), and I felt, as long as He had it laid on my heart and I was called to provide for them, I would follow through. And contrary to worldly belief, I believed with everything in me that if that meant going into deeper debt, as long as Christ was in it, He would provide a way out as long as I was faithful and obedient to Him.

If you wait until all of your own issues are gone before helping others, it will never happen. This is a trap that millions have fallen into, not realizing that our own sanctification happens as we minister to others. (Francis Chan, *Crazy Love*)

Through a sermon series, I would come to realize why I had such a burden to provide for these two brothers, even though it was costing me something. A church I would later attend, after leaving the church where I was currently youth pastor, taught a lesson titled "Goldilocks" in November of 2014. During a part of the pastor's sermon, he stated what it was like to have a *sacred concern*. I had never heard of the term sacred concern before, but it was stated as,

God gave me gifts, and these are the gifts that I believe I've been given, and these are the gifts that the community around me is affirmed, to God be the Glory to the service of others, may I use the gifts, and you'll know when you're using your gifts to the fullness because it'll cost you something! It won't bring you glory. When your gifts that God has given you have been redeemed for the greater good of His Glory and the service of others, your gifts will cost you something, and at some point, you'll be operating in your gifts and you will, through a sinful experience think, "I wish I wasn't gifted this way and wish that this burden wasn't on me"!…That's what happens to people when they surrender in fullness, and then it's just another thing to realize, oh yes, Lord, to you be the Glory! (Tommy Politz)

Weeping, and as tears flowed down my face in a complete overwhelming state, I now knew why I was gifted for this and displayed such a concern for James K. and Josh and, therefore, realized I had a sacred concern, and that it was costing me something. I somewhat grasped what a sacred concern was and have to admit before hearing this teaching, that, many a time (while going deeper in debt), I would say to myself, "I wish I wasn't gifted this way and wished it was not such a burden on my heart to provide for a couple of brothers," whom I met on the softball field on that hot summer day in May of 2009, but felt I had no choice than to be obedient to this calling.

CHAPTER 9

PREPARING FOR CHANGE

During the years of 2008 and 2009, they were economically tough for not only The Drawing Board but for many since the nation was struggling as the unemployment rate would increase. Jack and Sandie (TDB owners) seemed a bit concerned, which, in return, allowed me to me feel uneasiness financially, while working through what seemed to be a slow time in our industry. I was bothered by the slowness of the business a slight bit, but I always tried to trust the Lord that He would always provide during those tough times as well as the good times. I did begin to start feeling as if The Drawing Board may perhaps be struggling financially while overhearing some the conversations throughout the office. In the proceeding days, I started to have a feeling of uncertainty about the future of TDB. As it seemed to be struggling because of the housing market taking a dive, I wasn't sure what my future looked like with this company and began to seek other endeavors, in case something transpired and I needed to change occupations, which I thought were precautionary measures.

Without having said anything to anyone, and having just started my eighth year at The Drawing Board, I was approached by Gwen, whom I met at the church where I was youth pastoring. On one Sunday, without having said anything about feeling TDB was struggling, Gwen approached me about changing jobs and going to work at a local engineering firm. Having been at TDB the length of time I had been, I was skeptical about what to do, but it appeared like the right timing, and everything was right to look at changing jobs. I tried not to think too much into this and to just allow to happen what was designed to happen, but it was getting harder and harder to not get excited about possibly becoming employed at a large engineering firm. The requirements to fill this position were to have drafting experience, which I had, and to have a bachelor's degree, which I had.

Psalm 139:10–12

Even there your hand will guide me,
and your strength will support me.

I could ask the darkness to hide me

and the light around me to become night—

but even in darkness I cannot hide from you.

To you the night shines as bright as day.

Darkness and light are the same to you.

The requirements were there for me to apply for this company, and I was excited to work for a corporation rather than a small local business. I saw the opportunity to make more money, have insurance, 401(k), paid vacation, and I looked forward to working my assigned hours and going home. I typed up and generated a current resume and submitted it, with Gwen being a reference. A couple of weeks went by, and sure enough, I was called in for an interview, and two weeks later, I was employed at this engineering firm. This was a company that employs over 20,000 personnel and is a power plant design company with multiple locations across the US. "Let's focus on believing the promises given to us by God, on submitting to Him the fears that we have, and on surrendering ourselves fully to the work and will of God, the Holy Spirit" (Francis Chan).

I knew leaving TDB wouldn't be easy but felt it was something that I needed, and even some way, somehow, I knew the

Lord was in this. I gave notice to Jack and Sandie at TDB but assured them I would do all I could to help find someone and help with the transition as much as I could. Through the drafting program at the local community college I had attended, I met a friend named Kyle. After working at the surveying firm for a few months, I got him a job as a surveying tech there as well and was still on staff after I had left to become employed at The Drawing Board. It wasn't much later, after having left the surveying business, that Kyle would leave as well. He had gone through some family tragedies and was unemployed for quite some time. The first person I thought about filling my position at TDB was Kyle. I made a phone call to him, and he was eagerly starting to look for somewhere to work again and took no time to agree to become employed at The Drawing Board. I was slated to start at this engineering firm July 2 of 2012 but needed to get Kyle up to speed at TDB before then, with June 29 being my last day full time at TDB.

I had always wanted a career being employed by a company that had benefits, retirement, good pay, and be somewhere I could stay for twenty-five to thirty years and retire. I was walking into this new endeavor having these thoughts and already had it decided that I would probably end up retiring with this company as I'd hoped this would be my last place to be employed.

Now being employed with an engineering company made it a little tougher with the youth ministry, but I managed to make it work and still continued to be engaged as well as still trying to help out TDB as much as possible until Kyle was up to speed with the architectural and residential design. The more time that went by, the more Kyle was starting to understand and learn the job at The Drawing Board, which allowed myself to not be so engaged there any longer, which was hard. But it seemed to be taking care of itself as I was still plenty busy with my new career and being employed as youth minister.

Having been at this new company for a few weeks, I was invited to a Bible study, which was held during lunch once a week. I was quickly astounded by working for a company that engaged in a Bible study for their employees, therefore, it was a time for us to become an accountability group for each other and to participate in different studies each week. As I became more involved with different committees and events, I came to know a guy named Phillip. As I got to know Phillip better, he was someone who I quickly connected with and would become someone that I could go to for anything and would become close with from day to day at the engineering firm.

After getting to know Phillip personally over time, I came to find out that he was involved at a youth center for troubled teens. He had been going out there for many years and asked if I'd be interested in serving along with him and the team. I eagerly jumped at the opportunity, and after the initial visit and time of observing, I knew this was an opportunity I wanted and needed to be a part of. This facility houses troubled teens and youth from areas all around the area. The team I served with met every other week and shared a time of worship songs and teaching with these kids. During the time I served, although it was an unfortunate situation, I had two of my youth kids from my youth group. Walking into a teen correctional facility and seeing two of your own youth kids will rip your heart out of your chest, but knowing the Lord was with them during that time brought reassurance to me more than anything. The one thing that stood out to me, in and through this situation, was for these two adolescents to have their own youth pastor during what could've been the worst time of their lives; it was nothing but a miracle and God at work. Only the Lord knew I was needed at a church where I was called to do many things but also to be there for these two adolescents while they were placed in a correctional facility, while having me as a church team member. God knew exactly what they needed and who He was going to put in their lives during a time they needed someone familiar in an unfamiliar place.

We had been doing a new Bible study series that was released titled "Not A Fan" with the youth group at the Baptist church where I was youth minister. There were several of us from the previous Baptist church who were getting a study time and fellowship on Sundays but had no other day (in the middle of the week) where we were getting fellowship with each other and, more importantly, was lacking time with the Lord among each other. As good as this series was while doing it with the youth, I felt that us as young career people and singles would definitely benefit more as it dealt with topics like having a relationship with the Lord, a decision or a commitment, following Jesus or following rules, and taking up your cross daily. While we had twenty to twenty-five interested in doing a study like this, we had nowhere that could provide space or hospitality for this group to meet at each week. I had a teaching team lined up and people ready to attend but awaited a place to host us.

I sent an e-mail out to the Bible study group from the engineering firm (which was the group I had been meeting with for a few weeks now) and inquired if anyone was interested in hosting a group of people to their home one night a week to have a Bible study and do a video series titled "Not A Fan." I received a response back in a short amount of time from this friend of mine from the engineering firm named Todd. In the e-mail that he responded back with, he stated that he and his wife had been looking for a group to host in their backyard as they had a TV on the back patio and had just finished their backyard, getting it ready to be able to host something like this, but was waiting for a group such as this that needed somewhere to facilitate. We met eight weeks straight to do this study, knowing only God could have orchestrated this. Having not been at the engineering firm for too long, He had placed me at a company where I was able to do a lunch Bible study each week, and while getting to know Phillip, He led me to the youth center, and now, He was using Todd and his property to host a group of twenty to twenty-five young-aged adults to have a video series titled "Not

A Fan" in his backyard. It was a short six months while I was employed at this firm, but the Lord had His plan for me there and quickly showed me the purpose of changing jobs, but He also showed me Proverbs 3:5–6, "Trust in the Lord with all your heart; do not depend on your own understanding. Seek his will in all you do, and he will show you which path to take."

CHAPTER 10

DREAM CATCHER

I had been familiar with this Christian Motorsports team even years before I would go to work for Dream Chaser Racing and had always longed to somehow, someway be associated with this team. In 2008, this team would start their own in-house engine program and would become an owner/driver team, which so many others at the top were starting to do. This Pro Stock team earned their first win in Houston in 1996 and acquired forty-two Wally trophies and fifty-six No. 1 qualifier awards over the course of two decades of competing on the NHRA circuit. In all, they claimed two victories in the Modified category and forty in Pro Stock. They won the NHRA Winston Pro Stock Championship in 2009 and always seemed to finish in the top ten each year. While I was working for Dream Chaser (DC), we would be at different tracks testing, and I would take notice of and see this team in the staging lanes. This Pro Stock team never knew who I was, but my eyes were always on this team, only for the reason of how the team carried themselves on and off the racetrack. This allowed me to desire to be a part of this team someday as that had always been a dream of mine. After becoming employed by Dream Chaser, I got to witness firsthand what this team was like and what they were about. Between hearing this team share interviews during television interviews and hearing other racers talk about how this team was, I knew I had a longing deep inside of me to be a part of an organization such as this one. They would not only give credit to God after each round win but would always go further than that by saying, "I just want to thank Jesus Christ my Lord and Savior as not any of this would be possible without Him." It didn't take long to realize they were without a doubt a Christian organization and that all his success and fame was credited to the Lord. Not only did they give God the credit but made it known through television, radio, and announcements, that he was a born-again Christian and, to my knowledge, not any other race team made this known publicly as much as this race team did. Even after leaving the Dream Chaser Racing team toward the end of 2000, I would continue to watch this team while dreaming and yearning to be a part of this team someday.

On November 15, 2011, I sent the team a message:

> I am Jeff Fiedler from Amarillo, Texas, and have been talking back and forth with someone on your team over the past months. I had just asked him today if you all were to ever have a position become available or add a position, that I would be interested! I used to work for Brad Klein at Dream Chaser Racing here in Amarillo and enjoyed every minute of it but felt the Lord calling me somewhere else! To this day, it is still my dream to work for a full-time Pro Stock team but not seeking just any team! As I was chatting with Al this morning, I just told him that I couldn't imagine working for a team and Glorifying Christ at the same time! There isn't a team out there that is as forward about their faith and bold about it as you all, and wow, that is huge

to me! Like I said earlier, I am not actively seeking a position with any other employer or team as I love what I currently do, but you never know what doors the Lord is opening and closing. I have been with this company (The Drawing Board) that I work for now for nine years and currently a part-time youth minister and have been for two years, but I think I would REALLY weigh some options and do some praying if you guys were to ever have a position become available! I just sent this message for you to keep me in mind if you were to need someone and just want to congratulate you, guys, on a great 2011 season. As a brother in Christ, let me just say thank you for how you guys represent yourselves and the difference you guys make in so many lives!! Thanks for all you do and look forward to hearing back from you in the days ahead! Thanks!

November 15, 2011, team response:

> Jeff, things are up in the air right now. I'm
> not sure what is in store for us in 2012. We
> are praying for clear direction, many different
> options available at the moment, but first and
> foremost, we want to be in God's will. This is
> not our team but God's team! In saying all
> of that, why don't you send me a resume,
> and we can see what happens in the next few
> weeks and months. We covet your prayers as
> we seek God's plan for us and his race team.

November 16, 2011, Jeff's response:

> wow! Well, as content as I am doing what
> I do now, I have to say, "I am STOKED" at
> the fact that you replied and have asked for a
> resume! I am trying and doing my best to not
> get excited in case something doesn't work
> out and if the Lord has a different direction

where HE is leading me or us! I know that if I am in HIS will and that when Christ is Glorified, my life will be content, but I have to say that my heart and face glow when I do think about and talk about this opportunity with the few that I have, just seeking some guidance and input on this opportunity! It's awesome how the Lord has guided me along the way, taking me step by step to a point in my life where I am blown away with what HE has done and already can't help but think that HE has already used me in PS racing, now currently in youth ministry, and just thinking of the opportunity that may be in front of me now that I could be in a position to use both, and I dream and know how incredible that would be! I will be in prayer for you all as you seek the Lord for guidance and what it is that HE wants for the days ahead! Thanks for getting back with me, and I will get you a resume in the next few days! Thanks so much and am excited about whatever it is that HE has for us in the days to come!

January 11, 2013, message from the team:

Are you still interested in working on a PS team? If so, have something you might be interested in.

January 11, 2013, Jeff's response:

I am! What do you have?

Team's response:

I've got an opening if you think you might be interested, we can talk.

Jeff's response:

I am! I get off work at 11:30 and have a lunch
meeting after that. Could I get in contact
with you at 1:00?

Team's response:

Yes, that will work. Just give me a call at my
office, and we can talk.

wow, wow, wow, wow, wow, I have an interview with an
NHRA Pro Stock drag racing team—not only an NHRA drag racing team but the ONE NHRA team I've dreamed of working for even
back in high school.

I called the team that day and had a brief phone interview,
and the conclusion to the phone conversation was "you might
want to make a trip here just to check things out and see what
it's about." With much excitement, confusion, apprehension,
and feeling every emotion possible, I left on the evening of
January 11, 2013, and headed to this motorsports team head-
quartered in Broken Arrow, Oklahoma, to go interview with
an NHRA championship-caliber Pro Stock team. As I traveled

down the highway heading toward Broken Arrow, I had many thoughts racing and running through my mind. Thoughts like, *I just started a job with an engineering firm roughly six months ago, and I can't leave that. I'm a youth pastor at a church, and I can't leave that. I'm helping at The Drawing Board part-time. They would never forgive me if I left town and, therefore, felt that I couldn't leave that.*

Throughout the road trip to Tulsa, I would talk myself into doing this, and then five minutes later, I would talk myself out of doing this. I continued down the highway trying to just let go and wait until the next morning, which was when I would interview with the motorsports team. I walked into the door of the race car shop as two Pro Stock cars were sitting on pro-jacks (jack stands), with the transporter parked inside, where they were prepping race cars, the transporter, and getting ready to leave for preseason testing. I had a seat in the office, and we began discussing and what was looking to happen for the upcoming 2013 season. By the time I left, they had told me this was going to be a full corporate sponsorship and how another Christian organization was partnering with them for them to also be able to minister to kids at the race track; therefore, I would be able to perhaps lead some Bible studies at the races, along with being a crew member on the car and that I was slated to run the entire 2013 race season with this team. During the interview, I was told they had a house up the road about a mile or so and that I wouldn't be out much rent, if any, to live there in their guest house.

I left there feeling I shouldn't do this but couldn't help but think, *What if I don't? Where could it lead to? Am I going to regret not doing this if I don't do this? But I can't as I have so many other obligations in Amarillo.* With much wrestling and prayer, "I'm going to do this," one day, to "I'm not going to do this" the next day, after having talked with friends and family, I had agreed that I had too much going for me in Amarillo and that I was grounded there and thought I'd better stay where I was at because it's the "safe plan," and that was where I was comfortable.

Remember Benny and Gwen, a couple you recall from earlier. Gwen was the one who had approached me about going to work at the engineering firm. This was a couple who was close to the Lord and who I felt had godly wisdom more so than most in my life. Not knowing what to do, I went to their house and shared with them the opportunity I had been given and wasn't sure what to do with. They were right there along with me, knowing I had just started a new job with a company, and felt the timing to leave probably wasn't the best. As I left their house, I was feeling a little more at peace about staying in Amarillo but continued to have the "Jeff, trust me gut feeling" from the Lord. As more and more days went by, I felt the Lord speaking directly to me saying, "Jeff are you going to trust me through this and follow me, or are you going to follow your safety plan and not experience what I have in store for you?" Having just gone through the study "Not a Fan," which I spoke of earlier, I felt God was putting to the test if I were a "fan" or a "follower."

I had previously told my dad my plan was to stay in Amarillo as he reiterated, "I think having just started a new job that's what I would do, Jeff." That night went by, and throughout that day, I felt the Lord speaking to me stating, "Fan or follower" and "Are you going to trust me as your Creator or trust your own instinct?" By a couple of days after my interview, I had an overwhelming feeling of "I must go, and I must do this" after repeatedly hearing, "Jeff, you have to go!" By this time, it was January 14 or 15 of 2013, and they needed me there in Broken Arrow, Oklahoma, by the end of January. Analyzing so many scenarios and conversations I needed to have, they consisted of "How do I tell my church?" "I just started with an engineering firm, and now I'm leaving" and "I'm leaving The Drawing Board after they had just brought someone in six months ago after having been employed there a little over nine years." I knew I had a lot to get done, which included putting everything I own in storage and leaving Amarillo, Texas.

I walked into the place where I went to work each morning on January 16, 2013, where I knew I had some news to share. John and Matt were my two immediate supervisors, and I felt I needed to tell both of them at the same time, but with John's office being close to the front and Matt's being near me toward the back, I wasn't sure how to address the news to a company where, only six months ago, I was coming in for my first day. Well, beyond my belief, I looked in Matt's office, and John was in there; he had strolled by on his way back to his office and just happened to stop in. I immediately got out of my chair with what I wanted to be boldness, but I was full of nothing but fear of sharing the news. I shared the news with both John and Matt explaining, "I felt it was a chance of a lifetime and that it was something I had no visions of ever happening," but it did, and I felt led to move on and to end my employment with this firm. Both supervisors were extremely encouraging and stated, "Jeff you get to live this thing called life once, and we need to live it to the fullest, and when opportunities come up like that, we have to take them." They reassured me that I would be checked as a rehire if anything were to ever happen, that I would be welcomed back. Hearing those words from supervisors gave me even more confidence, believing the Lord was in this transition for my life in its entirety.

My next stop was my church that I would be leaving, and I felt a heavy heart for the twenty or so youth that I was leading. I dreadfully drove to the church where I was currently employed during my lunch break from work and broke the news. I explained it was something I had only dreamed of happening, and only the Lord could have allowed this, and I believed this was the next chapter in my life. As hard as it was to share, I felt a sense of peace and relief and that the worst was over, until I received an e-mail from the pastor.

Letter from the Baptist church pastor:

Jeff,

Sorry about my lack of enthusiasm concerning your decision, but I am really concerned if it is the right thing, right now for you. Initially, since you already said yes, I felt there wasn't much to say. However, there are some things I believe worth considering. First, less than a year ago, you and I prayed fervently for weeks regarding accepting the job at the engineering firm. All said, you believed God wanted you to move that direction. It afforded you opportunities to grow in your field of expertise, and it afforded you more time for your ministry with the youth. Now after only five days, you believe God is telling you that new career was wrong, and this is right.

Second, I am a firm believer that when God wants us to make life decisions, He does call us to trust Him, but also with the timing. You haven't had an opportunity to "feel" this out on the road to see if you are a good fit for them, and them for you. Perhaps, it would have been better to go to one of the events from start to finish and see. Did they offer that as an option for you at all? Do you sign a multiyear contract with them for this position? If so, what does it say about termination? Can they just decide without cause to let you go 6 months down the road? If so, any benefits? Also, are you bound to them for the contractual period no matter what? I am concerned about how quick this "train" is moving just like I was concerned about the addition of Brian and Emily with the youth. If this really is what God wants from you in the next chapter of your life, does it have to be decided in 5 days? If you're the one God wants there, could there not be time to fully investigate all aspects of it? I mean if they might hire someone else if you wanted a little more time to decide, where does that leave God in the picture?

I am especially concerned about the youth too. You are right about people coming in and out of their lives. It happens all the time, but now you go, and Brian and Emily go, leaving them with nothing to count on. They all thought Brian and Emily were going to come and plug in with them for a while. I truly hope and pray that your decision is the right one because it will ultimately be a blessing for you, and God will provide someone to lead our youth again. We will all grow through this. I hope you don't take this message as an affront or demeaning or malicious in any way. I am just concerned about you, as well as the youth. I will pray for you to know for sure what God wants. I love you, brother.

Letter from Baptist church worship pastor:

Dear Church,

I am writing today thinking of the impact that Jeff has made on our Youth group. Wednesday night in the Youth room, we were having a time of prayer for Jeff, and I asked the question, "How many of you did Jeff have a role in you accepting Christ?" Well, over half the hands in that group went up, and as I looked around, I remember many of the stories and baptisms that followed. When God is finished with someone in one place of Ministry and that person leaves, knowing that they helped people get saved while they were there, I believe they can leave, knowing that they did their job! Thanks, Jeff, for the tremendous job that you have done with our kiddos, and I can't wait for you to come back to town, visit us, and bring the race car by so we can try it out in the parking lot. We love you, man, and will miss you greatly!

I had quite a lot of reluctance after going through with this but continued to sense peace trusting the Lord and pressing forward to move to Tulsa, Oklahoma, versus staying in Amarillo. I stayed in constant prayer and prepared to say my goodbyes to friends and family and proceeded to move forward. As time to decide came, my flesh kept telling me, "This probably isn't a good idea," but the Lord kept affirming in multiple ways and laid on my heart, "Jeff, I've got you and trust me." All the while, I kept replaying repeatedly in my head that I had a chance to minister to teens and be employed by a professional drag racing team and knew the Lord could use this as this had been my heart's desire; therefore, it seemed as if I was living a dream and felt it couldn't get any better than the opportunity I had before me.

Having made up my mind, after I officially submitted my resignation letter to my current employer on January 18, 2013, was when it all became real. I progressed on by submitting my letter of termination for my apartment lease, No. 207, on January 16, 2013. I was informed to be in Tulsa as soon as possible, and I knew things had to move rather quickly for this to all happen. After renting a storage unit, moving everything I owned, and loading what I needed in Tulsa into my Tahoe, it was time to head to Tulsa, Oklahoma, home of a Pro Stock team I had longed to work with and for many years.

On the morning of Tuesday, January 29, 2013, I headed east for Tulsa. I was as energized as a kid in a toy store for the first time, while driving east with worship music, shouting all the while declaring, "God thank you, God thank you," and repeatedly feeling the Lord was telling me, "Jeff, thank you for trusting me." While it was incredibly hard to leave a town where I had been since June 1, 1998, it was like a thousand-pound brick had been lifted off me, and I knew great days were ahead.

Walking into the shop that same Tuesday afternoon after driving there, again there was the feeling as if this were a dream, and I couldn't seem to get a grip of what was happening; where I was involved in a career and race team that only my heart knew it wanted. After working at the shop for a few days, the days snuck closer to heading out west to Las Vegas, Nevada, for testing. The morning of leaving for testing started at 4:30 a.m., but I could not wait to climb aboard once again in the hauler and begin a lifestyle of traveling the road and ministering while doing it. We tested in Las Vegas. As things seemed to go well, we loaded up and headed into Pomona, California, where this would be the first race of the season. After four qualifying sessions, we ended up #1 qualifier as eliminations looked promising for us on Sunday. My duties included removing the driveshaft, rotating tires, packing parachutes, and being involved doing between-round maintenance on the car. We didn't fare too well on Sunday as we shook the tires first round and were quickly defeated, but with Phoenix coming up the next week, we knew Pomona was a great start and looked forward to the next one. We took a few days to wax and clean the transporter, stock up on supplies, and prepare for the next race by getting parked and setup for the Phoenix race.

The same as Pomona, qualifying went our way, and we ended up No. 1 after Saturday's final qualifying session with a best of 6.498 seconds at 213.13 mph. We entered the race Sunday morning feeling positive and upbeat and ended up in the final round. The opponent ran a slower 6.538 elapsed time at 211.99 miles per hour as she barely outran us. We had the quicker elapsed time of 6.520 at 213.74, but she was off the line first and got to the finish line by just a slim margin ahead of the Camaro we were running. This only having been our second race together as team, I felt to get to the final was quite an accomplishment.

Stoked and excited about the next race, which was two weeks away, we packed up and headed back to Broken Arrow, Oklahoma. The plan was to go back the way we came, which was through Amarillo on I-40, but after having learned of a massive eighteen- to twenty-inch snowstorm, we had to figure out an alternate route. We would have to drive a day or so out of our way going through Las Cruces, New Mexico, eventually to Dallas, Texas, and entered the Oklahoma area as I-40 was closed and would be for a couple of days. Driving for the two to three days we drove, I was already anticipating the next race, which would've been in Gainesville, Florida, from March 14 through March 17.

CHAPTER 11

My Mess, His Purpose

Rolling back up to the shop late that night that next Tuesday, after having been in the final on the Sunday prior, we pulled in the shop and started to unload luggage, which was when I would learn my dream I was living had come to an end. After a long road trip back to the shop, I jumped down out of the transporter, eagerly awaiting to find out where I would be living in Tulsa as they had stated they were working on a living situation for myself upon returning from Phoenix, Arizona. I was quickly greeted by the owner as he had flown back, and it was that night I was informed, on the evening of February 26, that things didn't seem to be working out with my new position, and they felt it was best to split ways. They stated, "Why don't you go back and get a hotel tonight and meet us back here at the shop at 9:00 a.m." which was on February 27 on a Wednesday morning. I was met, yet again, by the owners early that next morning as they apologetically stated, "Jeff, we just don't feel like you were a good fit for the position and that we'll need to move forward without you." Through their tears, they kept apologizing and reassuring me, "Jeff, you've done a great job, and we like you, but it just feels you're not a good fit for what we needed."

Psalm 139:13–16

You made all the delicate, inner parts of my body
and knit me together in my mother's womb.
Thank you for making me so wonderfully complex!
Your workmanship is marvelous—how well I know it.
You watched me as I was being formed in utter seclusion,
as I was woven together in the dark of the womb.
You saw me before I was born.
Every day of my life was recorded in your book.
Every moment was laid out
before a single day had passed.

In complete disbelief, my childhood dream was terminated and shattered, and as quickly as it started, it was now over. I had never been let go or terminated from a job and was in disbelief this was happening. I had left a youth group and a brand-new job, where I had only been six months. As crushed as I was, and maybe even a bit depressed as I couldn't imagine why and how this was happening, I knew I had to find another job. The morning after talking with the race team, they gave their condolences and said, "Jeff, I appreciate what you're about." Someway, somehow, that eased the pain of being let go, and I told myself, "At least, he knows what I'm about!"

As we saw earlier, my financial situation was not great, which I'll explain in more detail later, but I felt the motorsports team was going to put me in the right direction for not only my spiritual walk and life but also financially as I was taking home roughly $1450 every two weeks. I felt, without any type of living expenses as I was promised a great living situation and while being on the road quite a lot in hotels, this was the time to get my finances in order, and the Lord had a plan to release me from financial burden, which I greatly had now, facing the unknown with living expenses and many unanswered questions without income or a job.

The night of being let go from the team, as lost and hurt I was, I called one of my best friends, James R. (who helped me coach youths throughout the years and became a great friend), and inquired about staying with him until I could get some things figured out. I needed to figure out a living situation and decide what to do career wise. James R. quickly agreed, allowing me to live with him for the unforeseeable future, until I was clearer on the direction and what steps to take next. As I look back on this and remember how devastated and disappointed I was, it reminds me of Proverbs 18:24 which states that there are "friends" who destroy each other, but a real friend sticks closer than a brother.

Getting the opportunity to work for a race team was a dream I never imagined happening, and I knew that if I ever had that chance, everything else after that would not seem "good enough" so to speak. I saw that opportunity as being at the top and never imagined wanting anything else but to drag race with a professional team; yet to be able to minister while doing it was even more of an overwhelming event that would surpass my every dream imaginable.

I immediately got back to Amarillo, got on the computer, and started searching jobs. While searching, I never looked for jobs in Amarillo. All my belongings were in storage, and I thought, *If I'm going to leave Amarillo, now is the time to do it.* I didn't care to see anyone I knew or knew of my move to Tulsa as I knew they would question, "Jeff, how is the racing thing going" or "I'm so excited for your opportunity." I had so many thoughts that kept me from wanting to be out running into people I knew, so I elected to stay by myself for a while until I came up with the next plan for my life.

Having a Christian outreach company for teens associated with the race team I had just got released from, I became a little more aware of what that company did and what it was about. I felt a strong interest in working for this company that supported troubled teens and Christian camps throughout the United States and was interested in an area director position. I had several phone interviews and e-mail conversations with them during the first week of being back in Amarillo as I started to look at possibilities for this position on March 1, 2013. I worked night and day trying to get this position by sending in a resume, cover letters, personality profiles, and references. I had never been in such a mess from a worldly perspective, yet I felt closer to the Lord than I had ever before. I had been praying more than I ever had and truly seeking HIS will for my life for the days ahead as I felt completely lost.

CHAPTER 12

WHEN GOD SAYS WAIT

I was in contact with close friends and family during this time, attempting to get any insight from others regarding what I should do and shouldn't do during a time in my life that I'd never experienced before. My brother and sister-in-law had been trying to get me to come to Lubbock to get my mind off things and enjoy some family time and clear my mind. Not being in the best financial state (in fact, I was in quite a mess), I always turned down the invite with a "no" or "I just don't feel like it" as I just didn't care to talk about the future or answer any questions that people seemed to always ask. I finally gave in to driving to Lubbock and spending the weekend there.

We got up March 9, a Sunday morning, in preparation to attend church at Trinity Fellowship, which is where my brother and family had attended for quite some time now. On this Sunday, their head pastor was absent and had a guest speaker filling in. I'm trying to remember how I felt as this was my first Sunday back in church after getting the news of losing my "dream job," but all I remember thinking was, *I have got to find a job and get things back in order.*

Sitting down in the church pew after worshipping through song, the pastor walked out onto the pulpit and gave a brief introduction about where he would be headed through scripture and what we would be studying during the time of his teaching in the next thirty-eight minutes. He introduced his sermon with, "I'd like to invite you to turn to two passages of scripture, Isaiah, chapter 40, and 2 Peter, chapter 3. Today, the message is entitled 'When God Says Wait.'" My mouth fell to the ground in disbelief, and I couldn't even fathom what was happening. My eyes looked like an overflowing swimming pool as they were filled with tears running down my face.

Here I was, seeking a job with persistence and doing all I could do to go after the first job I was offered after losing the job of my dreams, then roughly a week and a half later, I attended a church service where I was hit with a guest speaker that opened with the words "When God Says Wait!" Overwhelmed and completely overtaken was an understatement. The longer he delivered the message, the more tears flowed out of my eyes.

He brought up scriptures such as Isaiah, chapter 40, verse 29 through 31.

> He gives power to the weak and strength to
> the powerless. Even youths will become weak
> and tired, and young men will fall in exhaus-
> tion. But those who trust in the Lord will find
> new strength. They will soar high on wings
> like eagles. They will run and not grow weary.
> They will walk and not faint. (Is. 40:29–31)

Throughout the whole message he delivered, he suggested examples of times where he tried to drive through jobs and situations where the Lord reassured him in several instances where he needed to wait. The guest speaker closed with this, "What God wants to do in you is more important to God than what you want God to do for you" (John Spurling).

After the invitation and the service concluded, we headed toward the parking lot to get in the car to head to lunch. With many emotions running through my mind and anxiously try-ing to get in the car to fasten my seatbelt, my brother looked at me and said, "Jeff, that message was for you today!" Without a doubt, on March 9, 2013, that message was divinely appointed for me. While driving home back to Amarillo, from the time I left the parking lot of Trinity Fellowship, I had never experienced that type of peace and true feeling of the Lord speaking directly to me like He did that day. I could hear him in my heart reassuring me by saying, "Jeff, just wait!" I did struggle days following that Sunday but knew I felt a peace come over me where I knew God had a plan for my life like I never had before, but I just needed to wait!

As I arrived back in Amarillo, I did my best to "wait on God" and be patient, but not having any type of job lined up or income coming in, it was a bit concerning, although I knew God has a plan. I continued to go after and pursue the Christian outreach company for teens, and while patiently waiting, I was advised on March 18, 2013, that others applying had extensive experience in this field and that they appreciated my interest and would be praying for God's favor and peace as I looked for direction in the days ahead. Feeling lost and unsure of what direction to go in next, I just continued to pray and do my best to just *let go*.

Through scripture, forty-three times in the Old Testament, God instructs His people to wait on the Lord. While we're waiting on God, "We want God's Blessing, but we don't want His timing. We want His penny, but we're not interested in His minute. We want His help, but we don't want His calendar" (John Spurling).

CHAPTER 13

IF YOU ALLOW HIM

I still had not been around the town of Amarillo much at all, fearing I would see someone I knew. I was afraid of individual encounters who would inquire about why I was back in Amarillo and that I would have to share that the thing I wanted and desired more so than anything else was only a reality for a very short while, therefore, I was back in Amarillo trying to figure out what to do next. I decided to go by The Drawing Board on a day toward the end of March and explain what happened and the situation I was in. Without any hesitation at all, they said, "Jeff, you know there is a computer not being used back there and that you are more than welcome to come back to The Drawing Board and start drawing." As nice as that seemed, I just didn't want to plug right back into The Drawing Board, but strangely enough, I had started to feel a peace from the Lord about being back there again and that maybe, for the time being, this was where the Lord was placing me. From that day forward, I got up each day giving it the best I had, although some days were tough. I continued to feel like there was not any way I would ever have the drive or passion for another career again as I had the career of my dreams, and I felt I had reached my dream after working at Dream Chaser. The difference was, I was no longer chasing my dream but had attained it, yet now had lost it.

I remained honest by giving The Drawing Board all I had and doing my best while I continued to feel this was where the Lord needed me. In my days at The Drawing Board, before becoming employed by the engineering firm, I always had the feeling of "What if maybe I owned this place someday?" I never had a full grasp of what that would look like, but I occasionally had that feeling "What would it look like if I were to own my own business?" As I continued to be back at TDB, it started to feel as though this was where I was supposed to be again. I had started to feel some vision and direction again, and as the future was undetermined, I started to get glimpses of what might be in store.

As I came "back to The Drawing Board," so to speak, there was something different about being back, and I almost felt as though, without anyone saying a thing, I was coming back as the office manager. I was handling a lot of the meetings, scheduling appointments, deadlines, and managing a lot of the financial duties that coincide with managing a business. While Kyle (who replaced me when leaving to become employed by the engineering occupation) was still employed by TDB, he was starting to talk with me about possibly buying the business. Initially, I was for the idea but truly never had a godly peace about becoming business partners with Kyle. We continued to work together for a while longer, both questioning about taking over the company or not. Kyle wanted to move the business location and change several things if we were to buy it together, which, I felt, would all be poor decisions since TDB had been in business since August of 1988 and at this location since 2000.

A year and a half had passed, and I still found myself happily employed at TDB. It wasn't long after Kyle had wanted to make many changes to the company that Kyle left to seek other opportunities. While I was relieved of the pressures to not become a business partner with Kyle, I became eager to find someone else to be a business partner as I knew I did not want to pursue the business-buying process alone. I believed I was not in any kind of financial status to buy a business on my own nor wanted the responsibility of being 100 percent sole owner. While this whole Drawing Board gig was starting to feel natural again, and I was feeling as if I was supposed to be there, I had many unanswered questions, doing my best to "wait on the Lord" and take one day at a time.

While waiting on the Lord, trying to rush and hurry God in every situation I came across, in the fall of 2013, I had the Lord lay on my heart to do a study with some college students. These students were not currently in church and were looking to be in a group to be held accountable and to be in a group where they could talk and share about what God was doing in each of their lives. Many of these students were in the youth group where I was youth pastor and had now graduated but lacked being plugged in an accountability/Bible study group somewhere. While still living with James R. in his house, his residence and backyard with tables and a firepit, with myself teaching, would provide a place to go and bring accountability and a study for this group. James K. was among the many that would attend, along with some of his friends. I had siblings from the softball team that I had coached and others that I had come across over the years through softball and ministry at the church where I was on staff.

James K., the adolescent who approached me about playing softball back in 2009, whom I had a sacred concern for, was now employed at The Drawing Board. During the time James K. was employed at TDB, he was in his second or third semester in the drafting program, majoring in drafting and in the thick of things in his study. James K. wanted to find a job in the drafting field and was highly interested in the architectural side of things. He thought there would be no better place to start than The Drawing Board. As he applied, the staff felt this was the next step to advance the company with someone young and excited to start a new career, which excited me to be able to work with one of my best friends.

James K. decided, shortly after working at The Drawing Board, this occupation wasn't for him. He had been in a profession before this where he was active, up and moving around throughout the day, but this job called more for sitting at a desk for eight to ten hours a day, and he admitted that the drafting career wasn't for him. After James K. exited The Drawing

Board, I tried to take one day at a time and allow the Lord to completely take over to lead and guide the days ahead.

Timothy, the designer that I had worked with at TDB from when I started there until 2009, had left The Drawing Board that year to start his own residential design firm. Timothy and Nathan (also someone who had worked at TDB prior to my employment there) were now business partners in their firm, Drafting and Design. I hadn't seen Timothy in years since he had left The Drawing Board, and he had no knowledge of me returning to Amarillo after working for the motorsports team, until I ran into him in the aisle of the grocery store. It was this encounter in the grocery store that seemed to change my plans in becoming a business partner, which I had always challenged myself to do before the age of thirty-five. As we started to converse and have visions, I was going to oversee all the business part of things, which is where my heart was, more so than designing. Timothy, Nathan, and I had lunch a couple times, but not near the amount of times that Timothy and I had late phone call conversations about the up and coming days.

The closer time got to again knowing I needed to tell Jack at TDB that I'd be leaving and going to work with Timothy, the more I wrestled with the decision. Timothy had worked for Jack for almost seventeen years, so they knew each other well. I had never been one to hide emotions nor hide what I had going on inside of me. The closer time got to signing the papers and becoming a business partner with Timothy, the more I had a knot in the pit of my stomach. After telling Timothy to go ahead and have Nathan put together a computer for me and get office furniture, I knew and felt no peace about the decision, but I wanted it so badly because it was the easy decision to make and felt it would suddenly benefit my *not so good* financial status.

The closer time got to sign the dotted line for the business venture with Timothy, it began to bring anxiety and a feeling of no peace. Jack from TDB, in some way, was able to sense something seemed off and approached me coming back from lunch one afternoon. Walking in The Drawing Board with all sorts of uncertainty on my mind, I heard the words, "Jeff, come here!"

Jack questioned, "Jeff, what's wrong as something doesn't seem right?" Jack, having no knowledge of me looking to become a business partner with Drafting and Design, looked at me. "Jeff, I know you, and I know them, and it'll never work between you all."

I can't remember a time where someone in my life had been looking out for me more and spoke the words, which I believe were only from the Holy Spirit. I felt those words spoken by Jack were so powerful that I decided on the spot to end all and any thoughts and desires to go work with Timothy at Drafting and Design. I had already started to feel this decision about Drafting and Design wasn't right, but it seemed like the thing I needed to do to get my life on track and, more so, to get my finances in order. Although when the Holy Spirit speaks through someone that is in tune with your life and looking out for the best for you, *don't ignore it!* God speaks through those around you and those that care for you, therefore, why do we or why would we ever ignore someone that is *intimately acquainted* with the Lord led by the Holy Spirit?

CHAPTER 14

UNSATISFIED

On the night of October 19, 2013, I was at the office helping James K. with an assignment he had due for his drafting class. While deep in thought, drawing lines, and doing our best to get this assignment turned in on time, I receive a text message that stated, "I hope your dad is okay. I heard he had a wreck out at the drag strip!" Without knowing any of the details or circumstances my mind began to race in various directions. I didn't know if he was in his personal vehicle, his race car, my race car, or what had happened. It wasn't long after I received the text, I had a phone call from my dad stating he had flipped and rolled my race car after being hit from behind and that he was okay, but the car was complete loss.

Not only was my car a loss, I also was at a loss for words when I heard the news. It quickly sank in that my drag racing career and hobby were both over, while it was just a few short months between getting let go by a race team and having my race car totaled. Not at all understanding why this had happened was completely mind boggling. It was a car that I had possession of since I was fifteen years of age, and at age thirty-four, I lost drag racing completely, both as a hobby and as a career.

While still waiting on the Lord to find out what my next move was regarding my career after getting back to Amarillo from Tulsa, I knew I needed to get back in church. Having been back so quickly from Tulsa, Oklahoma, and after receiving a not so supportive e-mail from my pastor at the church I was employed at just a few weeks before, I felt going back there probably wouldn't be a good choice, nor did I want to share a lot about what happened as it had been a roller-coaster month. I felt I needed to visit a place where I didn't have acquaintances nor knew anyone so that I could go and worship and to not have the feeling of needing to explain what had happened. I felt I needed to be somewhere I could just worship and heal from this whole—what I felt at this time—fiasco. On Sunday, March 16, 2013, which was the next Sunday after hearing the sermon "When God Says Wait," the Lord then led me to a Christian church. It was a very large church, and I heard the name referred to as Six Flags Over Jesus several times, but I knew a couple of friends that had attended there always spoke highly of this place of worship and felt that I would try it.

The series this church was currently in, which was the fourth part of five, when I visited that Sunday was titled "Unsatisfied." Again, I was definitely unsatisfied where I currently was in life and, again, felt overwhelmed how God knew I was unsatisfied and placed me in a place of worship that couldn't have been a better fit for where I was in life at that time. I continued to attend this church as I was passionately feeling led to become a part of this church family. It was exactly the place I was seeking as it was a place I could go and just worship freely without any pressures of being involved and was looking to rest in the Lord to see and hear what He needed from my life next.

As I attended for a few months, an up and coming series on *money* was nearing. I had felt compelled to be tithing while attending but continued to seem to fight that obedient act that God calls us to do. I was trying to get out of debt, buy a business, and had just returned home from what I thought was going to be a financial advantage with the motorsports team, which ended up being a financial setback. It seemed as if the harder I worked to get out of debt and to strive for this to happen, the further and deeper into debt I went.

CHAPTER 15

IT'S WORTH THE WAIT

Feeling as though a thousand pounds had been lifted off my back eliminating the Drafting and Design endeavor, doing my best trying to gain the passion and vision for TDB I once had felt, my mom ran into an old coworker of hers and an acquaintance we both knew. She so happened to run into Damon who was eating out, whom she hadn't seen in over ten years. They conversed for a bit as far as what my mom had been up to and then she inquired about what Damon had been up to. He stated, "I'm just working but looking to get into an ownership of a small business of some type."

While I was still unsure about making the purchase of The Drawing Board, knowing I wanted a business partner the entire time, something about this seemed like it fit just by only hearing of their conversation, having yet to talk to Damon about purchasing The Drawing Board. Damon and I went to dinner at a local restaurant in early 2015, and through that dinner and some other visits, I began to have a peace about the direction he and I were looking at going for the next year and our business venture. We had looked over some financial records from the previous year for The Drawing Board, but none of us knew exactly what TDB was worth or what Jack and Sandie would want for a business that had been in business since August of 1988 that Jack started. We stayed in contact throughout the days from when we met at the restaurant initially, until we finally made an agreement with Jack and Sandie and then proceeded forward purchasing the business, which was planned to transition over on January 1, 2016.

After having worked this particular morning in May of 2015, I went to lunch and told Jack that I was headed to lunch and would be back in a bit. I had previously mentioned to Jack (the current owner at TDB) that we were starting to get busy enough to need an additional designer. We would need someone that had previous home design experience and that would be able to come in and go right to work without having to extensively train. I mentioned this to Jack around the middle of April of 2013, and May 4, 2013, was when we had a new residential designer start. A girl named Rhiannon had come by while I was at lunch that day, and she shared with Jack that, after ten years, she was informed by her employer that the home design and build firm she was currently working at would be closing, and her boss would be retiring in the next few weeks. She immediately started seeking out other job opportunities, and The Drawing Board just so happened to be the place that was looking to hire the position she was pursuing. Keep in mind that The Drawing Board never put anything out as far as seeking this position as all I had done was just mention it to Jack, and a few weeks later, the Lord brought the person that was already trained in this field. Rhiannon understood roof design and how to design custom homes as she had been in this field the previous twelve to thirteen years and looking to go to work somewhere else designing homes.

While the plans were in the works to buy out The Drawing Board, I felt I was headed in a direction where I was feeling led, but at the same time, I was trying to drive my plans and path for the future more so than just "letting go" and letting Christ lead me. The closer the time approached to taking over The Drawing Board, I knew lots had to be done and discussed before we could reach an agreement of purchasing the business.

We hadn't gotten with Jack and Sandie yet as far as price for the business and knew lots of those details still needed to be taken care of. I could feel as though I was trying to drive my life in the path and direction it needed to go. I knew quite a lot had to be done during the summer of 2015 for Damon and me to be able to take over The Drawing Board in January 2016. I was starting to ask questions to Jack and Sandie about price of business and assets but never got a clear answer.

Anxiously trying to force this situation on July 12, 2015, I woke up at 3:00 a.m. in a cold sweat, with my heart beating out of my chest. I sat up in bed for a while hoping the feeling would dissipate, but it didn't after a few minutes, which felt like eternity. Josh had just happened to stay at my apartment that night, and I woke him, asking if he would just stay up with me until the feeling of my heart pounding passed. The longer I stayed awake to see if the feeling would go away, it seemed to worsen. The more my condition stayed the same, or may have of even worsened a bit, I told Josh that "I need to go to the emergency room."

I did my best to pray and ask the Lord to take away the feeling I was having, but not a single thing, at this point, seemed to help. Josh drove me to the hospital, and I walked into the hospital early that morning with a blood pressure of 160/108. I knew there was a problem when I was awoken by the pounding of my heart but didn't realize my blood pressure had escalated that high.

After running tests and getting results back, all came back normal except my blood pressure. I was sent home three hours later and advised to contact a cardiologist the next day for them to do a stress test and some further evaluations to what could have cause this episode. The medical staff at the hospital called in some blood pressure medicine and advised that I go by the local pharmacy and start taking that until I could see a cardiologist. I was scheduled to see a cardiologist later that week, which I was dreading, to go and to find out what might be found from the results. I was given a heart monitor to wear for several days while monitoring my heart rate. There were a couple of times where I had an irregular heartbeat, but not anything that the doctor seemed to be concerned about. A week and a half to two weeks later, everything seemed to be getting back to routine, and I felt back to normal.

While going to these doctor appointments, in the back of my mind, I felt I knew what caused this flare up that early morning on the twelfth of July. The whole entire time, I had trusted the Lord to guide and direct me through the transition from The Drawing Board, to the church where I was youth pastor, to the engineering firm, to the motorsports team, and then after the letdown with the racing team, I stopped trusting the Lord and tried to direct and create my own path. I'd never been angry, so to speak, with God, but to say I was disappointed in Him would have been an understatement—after having left a great job, a church where I loved being a youth pastor, and leaving a support group of friends! I was feeling as though I was tired of waiting on Him to show me the direction to take, not only for career path but also to attain financial freedom.

CHAPTER 16

LEFTOVERS

One of the studies titled "Leftovers—Leftover Money" was done on February 8, 2015, at the Christian church where I was currently attending, which was several months before the July medical episode that I would encounter. I was more convicted to start tithing after this series but doing all I could to relieve myself of debt. I continued to fight the temptation to tithe and to be obedient to what the Lord called me to do. The more I fought this battle of tithing and the more I would wrestle with finances, it resulted in anxiety and was now overflowing into other parts of my life.

It appeared everything else I was going after was a fight, and it felt as if I were fighting with purchasing The Drawing Board and all parts of my life. After the "Leftovers" and the emphasis that they had put on money, the Lord spoke to me and said, "Jeff, are you going to trust me, or are you not. You have two options at this point, either trust me with what I have given you and surrender all you have, or fight your way through it and know you're not going to win."

Completely broken just a short while after having made the visit to the ER that early July morning, with my pulse beating out of my chest, I decided, "Lord, I'm going to trust you and only trust you through whatever you bring me to. You allowed me to have an experience with a motorsports team that only you could've allowed, so why am I trying to drive through this stage of my life, when I know you know me better than I know myself."

I made a promise to myself and to the Lord, from that day forward, I would completely surrender everything and every part of my life to Him and no longer fight Him to drive my life. I promised myself that even this act of surrendering would include my finances and would begin first and foremost with tithing, which I had fought with for so long as I were shown completely different beliefs on this early in my childhood.

On August 2, 2015, I had my first tithe scheduled to come out of my account electronically, which would automatically be drafted out of my account so I wouldn't have the temptation of not tithing week to week. Once I admitted to myself everything

I had was the Lord's anyway, and I was cheating God out of the first fruits of my life, which therefore, I realized, *why is He going to trust me and bless me with more when I have not been a good steward with what I've already got?* I think we have this mind-set where we can give a part or a percentage of our lives to God and hold on to the rest. Holding onto my life in mainly the financial part of my life woke me up in the middle of the night and sent me to the emergency room because I wouldn't "let go" of something that was already His.

We ourselves are not impressed with "leftovers." When we have an option between a fresh meal versus a leftover meal, I bet we'd take the fresh meal. Were you ever that person when growing up that you had people you wanted to hang out with or be friends with, and the only time they would spend time with you is when they had no other friends around, and you became the "leftover" friend? How did it make you feel when you were a "leftover" friend? Not that God needs our money, but I wonder, when I was giving Him my "leftovers," how did that make God feel? I was giving God my "leftovers" but expected a blessing from Him each time I felt I was giving, yet my heart wasn't in the right place, and I knew the entire time I was giving just to give and had no obedience or heart motive behind it.

CHAPTER 17

FIEDLER MANNING, LLC

As time continued to tick away and pass quickly, I started to feel a bit of normalization set in. We were headed in the direction of buying Jack and Sandie out at The Drawing Board and, hopefully, on the path to reach my goal of owning a business. I had always told myself that I wanted to attain my own business at the age of thirty-five, but the takeover date for the business was set to January 1, 2016, when I would be thirty-six, so I would only miss by a couple of months.

Seth from the softball days, whom I met when he was seven years of age, was scheduled to graduate in May of 2015 and was starting to show interest in the drafting field. He attended the drafting program as well and quickly became interested in architectural and residential design. With it currently being Jack, Rhiannon, and I, we were starting to get busy enough to hire an additional draftsman. Rhiannon had settled in well and was progressing right along and getting better each day. Seth was enrolled in his first semester at a community college and had expressed interest in working for The Drawing Board. Not having anyone else to take with me in the field, I took random friends from time to time, and this time, it just so happened to be Seth. With him seeing and getting a glimpse of what The Drawing Board did, he became interested while still in high school. I ran this across Jack, and everyone agreed that he would be a great candidate for our next employee. Seth's first project was to lay out an existing large residential structure where a big addition was going to happen. Seth did an outstanding job getting this project laid out, and all quickly felt that Seth would be our next full-time employee at The Drawing Board, which he became that on November 9, 2015.

The day would finally come. After going to banks, meeting with CPAs, lawyers, and coming to a price agreement with Jack and Sandie, January 1, 2016, would be the first day of operation for the newly taken-over business, Fiedler Manning, LLC, doing business as (dba) The Drawing Board. Going into this head first, I knew I would now be responsible for employees and their livelihood. I knew I had no choice than to just *let go*, knowing I can't control any of this, and I told myself, "Why would I want to, knowing the Lord has done what he has so far," therefore, why would I even attempt to get in the way!

Entering the first week as a business owner, we already had payroll coming up and bills to pay, but since the July night the Lord got my attention, I knew that the Lord brought me to this point, and He would and will always provide, knowing I had to *surrender all*, including The Drawing Board, to a Lord that knows my every thought and my every desire. The Drawing Board went on; we got through our first year of business without any hiccups or roadblocks, and it went smoother and better than I could've ever imagined it going for our first year as a business.

CHAPTER 18

GOD KNOWS YOUR HEART

While working away at The Drawing Board and feeling as if things couldn't get any better; a builder contacted me about having a custom home to build and a spec to build. A spec home is a home a builder builds to sell without being a custom layout that an individual or family designs, versus the builder coming up with the layout and design of the home. This builder, being a contractor named Jeremy, was also a head of the 911 dispatch center in Amarillo, which is the dispatch center for police, fire, and EMS. I quickly became interested in knowing Jeremy. While being a captain at the local fire department seemed cool, the fact that he was head of the dispatch center seemed even better. I quickly thought to myself, *What if something were to happen through this where I could dispatch for the local 911?* While drawing plans for Jeremy for his spec and custom, I quickly became eager to know him and was curious about what he did and how things went at the communications center.

The more I got to know him, and the more our paths crossed, I asked if I could come observe some night, just to see what it was all about and to see what a 911 dispatch center was like. On the night I observed, which was entering the Fourth of July weekend, I had the privilege of observing on July 1, 2016. I got to observe with a call taker and listened to multiple 911 calls while at the communications center that afternoon into the evening. I wasn't so much interested in the call take position, but fire dispatch is what my heart was passionate about. After a couple more observation sessions, I inquired from Jeremy about a part-time position as a fire dispatcher on October 12, 2016. After texting Jeremy inquiring about the position, he responded back on March 20 of 2017, asking how many hours I would be available if this were to work out. I replied, "Around twenty to twenty-five hours per week is what I could be available for."

His response was "let me think about it as getting you trained is the tough part." During this process, seeing if this was even possible or not, he asked if I were available to come by his office to discuss the dispatch opportunity. He couldn't meet on that day we had planned, but he texted a lengthy text a few days later, Thursday, March 23 of 2017.

> Yet God has made everything beautiful for its own time. He has planted eternity in the human heart, but even so, people cannot see the whole scope of God's work from beginning to end. (Eccles. 3:11)

March 24, 2017, I got a text that read, I talked to my people this morning, and we are all open to trying that idea of training and part-time with you. I'll keep you posted on the next move, but could you come see me today?

I immediately replied with "yes, sir, and can be there at 8:30." I remember I wanted a chance at this part-time opportunity more so than I'd wanted anything in a while, probably as much or more than the racing endeavor. I not only wanted this but felt called and that the Lord needed and wanted me there. I remember praying on the way to that interview that morning, "God, please allow me to get this job as I feel that *I can be light in a dark place* and help others in the time of need."

I walked into the communications center with great excitement yet apprehension as I felt I wanted this so badly and was afraid of something not working out. As I went into Jeremy's office, we began to talk about the position, hours that needed filled, and the words spoken out of Jeremy's mouth during the interview were, "Jeff, I'm excited for you to be here and feel like you can be *a light in a dark place.*"

He doesn't know, to this day, that I prayed those exact words, but when I got to my car to leave and head back to The Drawing Board, I was overcome with emotion as I knew the Lord was in this and that I would more than likely become a fire dispatcher, which I had longed for since I was nine years of age, carrying around my scanner!

I was advised to get my application in March 29 of 2017, and that a typing test, a hearing test, and a polygraph would be the next steps to being employed at the dispatch center. Through all of this testing, on May 31, 2017, I inquired when training would start, and June 1 2017, I received the text I'd been waiting for. Jeremy shared the text with me that stated, "Just got the official word…you are a green light, welcome!"

If you remember, to the day nineteen years ago, was when I moved to Amarillo, Texas, and nineteen years later, I would become a fire dispatcher. This would be for the local dispatch center. Therefore, after dreaming of being a fireman, listening to scanners, and logging calls back since I was roughly nine years of age, it became life.

What excites me about this is that the Lord knew I wanted to be a fireman, He knew I treasured logging calls into spreadsheets, He knew I was excited about fire trucks, He knew I was passionate about dispatch, and years later, God would open a door through The Drawing Board and allow me to run across Jeremy and for me to again realize "God knows my heart better than I know myself." Through the drafting business that I tried to leave a couple of times, from going to an engineering firm to drag racing, I would meet a fire captain who was a builder and so happened to be the fire captain that was employed at the 911 communications center, who has been an encouragement and a man of God for me even today. He has shared scripture with me, shared inspiration with me regarding different circumstances, and what excites me most of all was that he followed through with God's plan to bring me to dispatch!

I'm not sure whether you are reading this book as a believer or a nonbeliever in the Lord. If you are a nonbeliever, my hope is that after having read the above paragraph, your views will begin to change about the Lord wanting you to be intimately acquainted with Him and knowing, without a doubt, He has such purpose for your existence and life on this earth. He didn't put you on this earth to "just exist." He didn't put you on this earth just to "barely get by" or "be average." In fact, your life is God designed, purpose-intended, and significant for God's purpose to use you for His glory.

If you've ever bought and put a puzzle together, you'll be able to relate to this. As you walked down the aisle at the store, looking for the puzzle desired to put together, you may see many types yet stunning images on the puzzle boxes being looked at. It's not the pieces in the box that made you buy the puzzle, but it's the magnificent image that is on the box front that grabbed you and got your attention enough to purchase the puzzle from the shelf. The first step in putting a puzzle together is getting home and dumping each piece out onto the kitchen or dining room table, preparing to create this same image that was on the box front. While rummaging through the pieces, hoping not any one piece is missing, you begin to place piece by piece into the puzzle. Putting this puzzle together, you cannot help but realize each piece has its own unique shape and design and is perfectly created and made for only one place where each piece fits for its purpose.

If this puzzle you are putting together is 500 pieces and you get down to having it completed and lack 1 piece because it is missing, the other 499 don't matter; it's still missing 1 piece and won't create the magnificent image on the box you so badly wanted to create. It's the exact same thing with us and our lives. Each of us are messed up and sometimes may feel as though our life is a disarrayed 500-piece puzzle, but with the Lord as our Creator, there are no missing pieces. We just need to allow Him to put us together. Your life is a part of His puzzle, and without your life, His puzzle isn't complete. After you complete a puzzle and set that final piece, you take a step back and would probably say to yourself, "Wow, look at that!" or "What an incredible picturesque image that is!" Whatever it is, you probably had a sense of accomplishment and a feeling of "Look what I put together."

I believe the Lord has that same thought about your life and my life if we'll just let Him guide us and direct our lives to create His puzzle while using you and I for the pieces. Your life is so vital, and I believe God's perfect puzzle and plan includes you, where in the beginning you may feel like jumbled puzzle pieces, but in the end, after you've allowed Him to put your life together, I believe we can look back at our lives and say, "Look what God did with my life." Truth is, He loves you too much to leave you the way you are and has a love for you that you and I will never understand, but knowing He is the source of love and the definition of love, know that without a reservation, our Lord God wants the best for each of our lives.

If God is calling you to a purpose, don't stare too long at the obstacles. Don't let fear determine your destiny. Instead, ask God for wisdom. Pray for the Lord to create a plan for your life and take that first step toward what you feel He might want for you. God will move the obstacles one by one as you move and trust Him to live out His plan for your life.

CHAPTER 19

GOD AS YOUR SHIELD

While in the middle of our third year at The Drawing Board, I still tried to keep up and stay in touch with a few of those that remained close to me from the engineering firm. I remained in touch with Todd through the youth center. I continued to see Phillip at the Christian church that I started to attend back in March of 2013 from week to week. Chris was the one I remained in contact with, mainly because his daughter worked for us at TDB as a receptionist, so I remained in contact with him through her from time to time. It was through these individuals, in the spring of 2018, on May 29, that I learned the local engineering firm would close its Amarillo location and that everyone employed with this company, where many were employed for many years, would either lose their job, be forced to retire, or forced to relocate to a different location.

The Lord will keep you from all harm—he will watch over your life; the Lord will watch over your coming and going both now and forevermore. (Ps. 121:7–8)

Now knowing this location would close in Amarillo, relocating to Tulsa, Oklahoma, for a short time now seemed for the purpose of protecting me. Had I remained employed with the engineering firm, I would've been forced to relocate or change jobs at a moment's notice. I would have bypassed an opportunity with a race team, which would not have been an opportunity the next year (2014) as the team hung their helmet up and retired from drag racing and Pro Stock racing after the 2013 season.

When it comes right down to it, don't ever ignore God, which is that small voice sometimes whispering, but when He speaks, He will speak to you stronger and heavier than any person on this earth. The more I tried to stay at the engineering occupation (mainly for the reason I had people telling me "Jeff, you just started a new job, and at that, a good job, and not sure how you could give that up"), the more I felt the Lord speaking to me saying, "Jeff, trust me, and not them." Wow, now looking back and seeing how the Lord removed me from a company that He knew would close this location encourages me, and I hope it encourages you to trust Him even when it doesn't make sense to you or those around you.

Looking back and seeing the timing of everything, God gave me an opportunity to drag race with a professional drag racing team, to come back and buy a business, allowed me to have a divine appointment with a fire captain, and bring me to a dispatch center, which I feel was a calling to be a light in a dark place.

I am going on almost three years with the communications center, now trained to be a fire and EMS dispatcher. Even through the darkness of the center, I can see the Lord in and through this place. I can feel a work being done in and through those that recognize Christ as the ultimate physician and healer through situations, although most see it as "being lucky," yet know God is not a God of luck and is so much bigger than being "lucky." The Lord is part of each call and each circumstance in that room, and it is only of the Lord to see miracles revealed from time to time through circumstances, like when people start to breathe again or their heart starts to beat again or someone just happened to find this person at the right time. Many believe that it's a coincidence, but there are no coincidences with the Lord. I believe they are all divine appointments, therefore, it reveals the Lord has it all in His hands only through His timing and purpose.

We are now entering our fifth year of business into the year 2020, which has been an incredible ride so far. I've had clients state that they were praying for us as God has been present in and throughout this business from the day we opened the doors. The Lord has provided financially, abundantly, far more for the company beyond my imagination. He has provided employees needed with abilities only He could provide with. We are in a profession where there isn't a large amount of people that do what we do, but He has provided the people needed that have the gifts to provide for the company. This also applies in life. Christ gives us qualities and gifts needed to complete His plan and purpose. Refrain from second guessing and doubting how you are made and created. God poured exactly the gifts into you needed to fulfill your life and serve other people to bring God *glory.*

I knew you before I formed you in your mother's womb. Before you were born, I set you apart and appointed you as my prophet to the nations. (Jer. 1:5)

Christ created you for His plan to be lived out in and through you, therefore, don't drive your life when you're not the driver. (Jeff Fiedler)

As we go through this life, we are just a passenger while we're on a track, while God is the conductor. We wouldn't get on a train and head right to the front wanting to drive as we wouldn't have the knowledge of guiding and directing a train; therefore, why do we feel that we know what is best for our lives over the Creator. When we create something, we know every detail and intricate part of what it needs to operate and work to its maximum potential. It's the same as God has created us. He knows every intricate part of our lives that makes us work and operate fully to our abilities, I believe, to fulfill our hearts desires but, mostly, to bring Christ *glory* in and throughout our dash. The dash (-) represents our life. We each have a date we were born and will have a date when we leave this earth, and there is a dash in between those dates. As soon as you're born, you have a date and now have a dash. My desire is to live out that dash to the maximum potential He has planned for me because that date at the end after the dash could show up when you and I least expect it, yet God knows the date and even to the second of when our time is up here on earth.

CHAPTER 20

FINANCIAL GAIN

Having paid off my personal loan as of September 2, 2017, I was feeling I was getting things paid for and having a peace and direction for guiding and directing my finances. The problem I was seeing was I would get one thing paid for and the other thing (credit card) was starting to rise. As of August 2018, I still owed $19,275.19 on my credit card. Looking back and knowing I had a sacred concern for James K. and Josh, it did cost me something. It cost me going further in debt, but don't think for a second going further in debt cost me a hospital visit. Not having been obedient to the Holy and Mighty God that fearfully and wonderfully created me caused my hospital visit which, I feel, was how the Lord got my attention and said, "Jeff, stop fighting with me and trust me."

There were many times, like I emphasized before, I had wished I wasn't wired this way, and like the Christian church pastor I currently attend stated in the "Goldilocks" series that through a sinful experience, I had wished I wasn't gifted this way because it's costing me something. In a much different scale, Christ going to the cross cost Him His life. Jesus willingly and knowingly went to the cross to die a death that not any of us can even fathom; therefore, if we're going to be a "follower" and not a "fan," shouldn't our life cost us something as well? If it took me going into debt to see not only James K. and Josh's lives change for eternity, with the eternal impact they have made on so many; why would it not be worth it?

> Then Jesus said to his disciples, "If any of you wants to be my follower, you must give up your own way, take up your cross, and follow me. If you try to hang on to your life, you will lose it. But if you give up your life for my sake, you will save it. And what do you benefit if you gain the whole world but lose your own soul? Is anything worth more than your soul? (Matt. 16:24–26)

I never wanted nor thought I'd be in the kind of debt that I was in, but I never once felt as though God wouldn't get me out of the situation, if it were His desire for my life. I was never thankful to be in the position, but I always knew that if it was God's will, I would get out of the circumstance of being a slave to my debt. I know some believe that it's not biblical to owe money or to be in debt, but for my life, and going back to the sacred concern, I believe with everything in me that God allowed that to happen in my life for a couple reasons.

The first reason being that the walk that I had with the Lord was to cost me something, and I knew that when I got out of it, that only God would get the credit. The second reason was to show the cost of God's love. Those I was showing love to didn't know I was in debt nor did that even matter, but the only thing that mattered was to show love to them during a time they were lost, and I could show them something they didn't understand. I didn't understand and still don't understand that when I'm called to do something for someone, while feeling that I was struggling myself, how could I help someone else when I myself don't have it altogether? You have a way of reaching people no one else can reach because of the unique ways God has gifted and wired you.

So I know what you're thinking; "The world around you and I, so to speak, would probably look at this and not approve of going further into debt to help two brothers" when, at the end of the day, they were cared for and loved by a sister that took them in and treated them as her own when she didn't have to. Although feeling she didn't think she could take on and adopt her two brothers at the time of the passing of their mother, while she was twenty-one years of age, she pressed forward and did an incredible job. Their sister has stated to me many a time, "I thank the Lord for placing you as a leader and godly figure in their lives while growing up." Now knowing the Lord gave me a sacred concern for these two, knowing it would cost me something earthly, therefore, there is nothing worth more than your soul, which puts earthly versus eternally in perspective!

We've got to realize that we are only here on this earth for a very short time, and I feel if you have a sacred concern for someone or something while on this earth and don't follow through with it, just know you might be the person God is try-ing to use to make an eternal impact on someone through your life. Don't seek happiness on this earth; seek *joy*, and contrary to what the people around you say or advise, there is no one or nothing on this earth that will overcome the feeling of having a sacred concern. If you are following through with your calling and being obedient to what the Lord wants you to do with it, I can promise you it will *cost you something* and that we can't shy away from it even though most in the world will state, "You shouldn't help them or do that for them!"

We've got to interact with nonbelievers with an attitude of showing them Jesus before they'll come to know Him. If we do not fulfill the plan that God has created us to live, it won't be a fulfilled plan lived out for God through you, if you are looking for comfort on this earth. I'm not sure where these brothers would be had I not lived out my sacred concern to the best of my abilities. Feeling as though I did the best I could with what I had, I got to witness something that made the cost all worthwhile, and that was seeing James K. and Josh give their lives to the Lord that October, on that Wednesday night, in 2009.

From that incredible night, I can now rest knowing they'll spend eternity worshiping a Savior that only you and I have because it cost Him something, which was His life, for us to be able to have a relationship with Christ. We are most like Jesus when we love everyone, and how will someone ever know a God that loves them when we don't show them the love that He has for us? There are lots of things we're wired with; I feel we don't even understand ourselves. One thing I'm wired with, and even myself doesn't understand fully why I'm like this, is that I have a desire to love everyone around me and to get anyone around me to love me. I've thought a lot about those who aren't easy to love, but that doesn't make me want to stop trying to love them, even though it would be easier from only a worldly perspective. It's my prayer that the people of God would love one another so well that the world would see us and say, "Something is different about them." Love one another with kindness and compassion. Not only will you be obedient to God, but you'll also give the world a glimpse of hope that's in you.

If I can get them to love me, I have a chance at getting them to love my God, but if they don't love me, I'll never get the opportunity to share God's love, and the possibility arises that they will never experience an unconditional everlasting love that they cannot fathom until they experience it.

As of November 15, 2019, I was completely out of consumer and credit card debt. The different roads that I've tried to take transferring credit balances from one to another, paying one credit card payment to cover another, and doing all I could to lower debt was doing nothing but increasing it. There are many scenarios that played in my head—if I were to do this, this would happen; if I were to do that, that would happen—but until I completely surrendered my finances to the Lord, not any of it were going to be taken care of. I don't want you to see this only as a financial gain but only as a steward and a surrender gain. You can't just surrender one-fourth, one-half, or three-fourths of your life; you must surrender the WHOLE part of it. I would have never thought that "just" tithing and giving would bring a peace and a new life like I've never experienced, but it has. There were definitely times where I wasn't a good steward of His things and money, in fact, up until that day on July 12, 2015, which was what got my attention, I wasn't a good steward, and I even struggled after that day as this is all a work in progress. I still haven't mastered it yet, but I thank the Lord I'm not where I was ten years ago, five years ago, or even yesterday because God knows my heart better than I know myself.

Even though I was not obedient with tithes and offerings, His possessions nor anything that was already His, He loved me through it all, which never lessened nor will ever lessen. I can't foresee the future and don't know what's going to happen tomorrow, but I can promise, having lived out of His will versus now doing all I can to line up my life mainly financially, I will continually only trust Him with my finances. The Word says in Matthew 6:24,

> No one can serve two masters. For you will hate one and love the other; you will be devoted to one and despise the other. You cannot serve God and be enslaved to money. (Matt. 6:24)

I would have been much wiser had I learned this at an early age, but I am so thankful I can now live on in my forties and beyond serving only ONE MASTER, and that master will be JESUS CHRIST as there is no other way to live, which will bring peace and life like you'll never understand, not unless you completely surrender and give it all away and remember not any of it is ours or yours anyway.

CHAPTER 21

FOLLOW THROUGH WITH HIS PLAN—HIS PLAN HAS PURPOSE

Getting to baptize James K. and Josh was something I'll never forget, getting to witness the spiritual fire they had as new Christians. The next first for me I would get to experience was getting to officiate the marriage of James and Kaitlyn. On September 23, 2017, I had the honor and privilege to be part of James K.'s life yet again. As I witnessed James placing the ring on Kaitlyn's finger, and vice versa, I couldn't help but think about how much the Lord loves us.

Even as much as James K. loves Kaitlyn, as the ring signifies a representation of how the love for her will never end—a ring is circular and has no end to it, which is what marriage should look like—but it is more how God's love never ends for us no matter the circumstances. Think about it; He willingly died on the cross for your sins, taking the chance of you not loving him back. As hard as that is to imagine, think how we only do things for people, mostly because we love them, or they love us back. What would it look like if you got up tomorrow and thought, *I'm going to do something for someone that not only doesn't love me but doesn't like me?* Showing someone the Lord before they know Him is all we can do for someone to come to know Him, but they must witness and see what He has done in and through us first.

As great a time as this was in James K.'s life to now be married, it was hard to see this take place. James K. had been a big part of my life since seeing him out on the practice field that day at that elementary school prepared to come play softball, but what he wasn't prepared for was the eternal difference that was going to be made through this divine appointment. James K. will now spend eternity with Christ because of the divine appointment that James followed through with, even though he believed he was just coming to a softball practice.

CHAPTER 22

HOPE IN PRESENCE

I had heard about a concert in Lubbock and had several friends asking if I was planning to attend. I had originally planned on going with someone, but the closer the concert time got, the more I felt led to go alone. I looked at tickets numerous times, just to be sure that tickets were still available. As time got closer and closer, I decided to go ahead and purchase a ticket, but only one. I had a couple trying to pressure me into going with them, but I always replied, "No, I'm just going to keep my options open as I do not want to commit to any plans regarding the concert."

The closer the time got to going, which was on a Friday, April 26, 2019, I started to feel as if I needed to go alone. I didn't want to attend the concert alone but started to feel almost conviction to attend with anyone else other than myself. After work on this date, I got in my truck and headed south to Lubbock. It was a great time of worship and prayer throughout the two-hour drive. I pulled up to the Spirit Arena with excitement yet reluctance as I was walking with thousands of other people, yet was alone. I walked about halfway around the arena and saw a section that was sparse and wasn't as crowded as most of the sections were. I navigated to my seat and quickly began to feel the Spirit fill this place.

> The truth is that the Spirit of the living God
> is guaranteed to ask you to go somewhere or
> do something you wouldn't normally want or
> choose to do. (Francis Chan, *Crazy Love*)

About halfway through the concert, a couple of adolescents, probably sixteen or seventeen years of age approached my aisle. As I was on the end, I had to allow them to go by me so that these two could get to their seats. We worshipped a while longer as I sat down for a moment and allowed the Lord to speak to me and for me to be "still and quiet" to hear the Lord and just spend one-on-one time with Him. As the service was ending, with only a few songs remaining, these same two young men trying to get by earlier to come to the service were now trying to get by to leave. One went by and then the other one made the motion to get by but hesitated as if he was going to speak to me. He came up to me in close proximity as the worship artists and all in attendance remained worshiping and carrying on, while it seemed this young man was going to have a conversation with me. He leaned into me, put his hand on my shoulder, and shared, "Hey, man, I can't help but notice you came alone tonight, which I think is awesome and says a lot about you, and seeing you here tonight challenges me to take a step of faith and lead even though it could be doing it alone."

As he was getting by me to leave the concert, I felt the Lord bring a peace over me about being there alone and felt the Lord speak, "See, Jeff, I had a purpose for you coming alone tonight, and don't ever doubt me when I have a divine appointment for your life.

I share this because even though we're alone and feel alone, God is always there by our side to guide and direct us of His *glory* even though it's uncomfortable. If I would've known going to this worship experience what was going to happen, I wouldn't have hesitated, but it took follow through and post obedience to see His plan lived out. Having faith the Lord is going to do something in your life and show you a divine appointment, it isn't ever easy to trust the Lord solely. Trusting the Lord while believing alone especially makes it difficult, where no one knows, but I have figured out that when you trust Him and are obedient to His calling and purpose, your life will have fulfillment and be a treasured possession by the Creator of the universe. As it states in Exodus 19:5, "Now if you obey me fully and keep my covenant, then out of all nations, you will be my treasured possession. Although the whole earth is mine." Christ will cover you with a peace and reveal purpose to your life even when you don't understand. As the worship service continued for a bit longer, I became overtaken by His presence and just that the Lord will always reveal Himself to us, trusting Him and not second guessing His purpose for our lives.

As I was in the middle of writing this (what I thought would be for my own reference and to share with those around me), I started to feel this might become a good read to share with believers and non-believers. As the Lord started to lay on my heart to look in the direction of getting this published, I began inquiring to just a few of those around me about how to get a book published. I had never done this before, and I was clueless about how to go about this process. I don't have any close acquaintances that are into writing or had books published, therefore, didn't have much of any direction on the topic.

Psalm 139:17-24

How precious are your thoughts about me, O God.
They cannot be numbered!
I can't even count them;
they outnumber the grains of sand!
And when I wake up,
you are still with me!
O God, if only you would destroy the wicked!
Get out of my life, you murderers!
They blaspheme you;
your enemies misuse your name.
O Lord, shouldn't I hate those who hate you?
Shouldn't I despise those who oppose you?
Yes, I hate them with total hatred,
for your enemies are my enemies.
Search me, O God, and know my heart;
test me and know my anxious thoughts.

Point out anything in me that offends you,
and lead me along the path of everlasting life.

On Saturday, September 14, 2019, I had gotten up and around, taken a shower, and was preparing for the day as I needed to catch up on some things at the office before going to the communications center at 3:00 p.m. I had dried some towels in the dryer the night before and needed to get those folded and some laundry changed out before I left. I had the thought of going to the office and getting other things done instead of laundry but thought, *I'll go ahead and get laundry out of the way so that I can get some other laundry going while I'm doing the other errands that needed to get done before 3:00.*

I removed the towels from the dryer and placed them on the couch. While I'm not much of a television watcher nor ever have been, but this certain morning, I decided to go ahead and power it on while I folded the towels, curious to what was on. I flipped through a few channels before finding Air Race World Championship, which came on at 10:00 a.m., and it was only a few minutes shy of 10:00 a.m. I knew I wouldn't watch this long as it was just to satisfy while getting the towels folded. I accepted the respected channel and turned to this programming, and when I did, there was a commercial on. I'm not sure what the commercial was before the commercial I'm about to tell, but just a few seconds after having the television on, a commercial came on, and I heard the words "Christian Faith Publishing" (CFP). I quickly became attentive to the television; where before it was mainly for background noise, now I felt the Lord was speaking to me. Through the quick thirty seconds this commercial lasted, I learned where and how to get a book published, edited, critiqued, and the contact information for CFP. I couldn't believe what I was hearing or watching and seeing right before my eyes. This was something I had never seen advertised in all of my years watching television and believed that only at this time, on this day, in the few minutes I had the television on, that the Lord revealed to me the next step to take in getting this book published and out to make a difference in millions of lives. There were many things I had planned to do on this particular day, but the Lord had a different plan, and that was to stop me with what I had planned to and show me what I needed to do in order to learn of this book publishing company called Christ Faith Publishing.

CHAPTER 23

CHANGED FROM THE INSIDE OUT

While trying to hurry God up, while I was being told "When God Says Wait" from John Spurling, he stated, "What God wants to do in you is more important to God than what you want God to do for you." Now that you are near the completion of this book, I hope you feel inspired, encouraged, driven to live for Him and, most importantly, know there is a God that died on a cross for you that loves you so much that He sent His One and Only Son to die a gruesome, painful, and unfathomable death to give you and I life and a relationship with Him.

When you think God doesn't care for you or about you, remember this book. There wasn't any part of this book that didn't have a "divine appointment" attached to it, where God didn't have my life mapped out perfectly to allow the desires of my heart. Remember you have a GPS wired in you and remember who that is and that He can see the whole picture in a much bigger view versus our narrow-minded earthly thinking. The world and the nonbeliever(s) around you will never understand your thinking or your actions as you live for Christ, but there is no life compared to a Christ-like life being directed by the GPS. God will change your circumstances while being unsatisfied, but He may require you to wait on Him and know He first needs to change you before your circumstances change. The "fan" of Christ won't understand this, but the "follower" will!

> When you humble yourself, you get lifted up; when you empty yourself, you get filled up; when you lower yourself, you get exalted, and when you forget yourself, you get remembered. (John Spurling)

What is it that you're waiting on the Lord for? Are you in a season of waiting? Maybe you are looking to attend a college but not sure what to major in. Maybe you are single today and wanting to be married. Maybe you are in a career where you do not feel comfortable in and want out. Maybe you are in a financial crisis and want out of it. Even through each of these scenarios, many of which I've encountered, knowing Philippians 1:6 is the only way I held on through all these triumphs and trials. This scripture states "And I am certain that God, who began the good work within you, will continue his work until it is finally finished on the day when Christ Jesus returns."

Growing into a deeper relationship with Him will override any of the struggles and troubles you have or are currently encountering. He won't do it immediately, but don't give Him the "leftovers," and know He will change you from the inside out!

CHAPTER 24

TRUSTING HIM IS
THE ONLY WAY

All throughout these events that I've shared throughout this read, multiple people have asked me multiple times "What are you going to do?" Whether it was during my parent's divorce, a job, career change, and the move from Amarillo, Texas, to Tulsa, Oklahoma, people often wondered and questioned me, "What are you going to do?" While I was in the transition stage of deciding whether to buy into a drafting business or to do a buyout, I was being asked, "What are you going to do?" People around us, friends, and family, always seem to want answers and want to know exactly what is going to happen, especially through transition when sometimes, we don't even know ourselves while we're waiting on the Lord!

Even through adversity, God can work through any situation and create good out of it. My parent's separation was not a good thing necessarily and yes, it is still hard at times, but had my mom not been in the situation she was in, I would not have been able to leave Hobbs and move to Amarillo in the timing that was planned. I'm not saying, "Go, get a divorce" because God will use it to the good of His glory, but what I am saying is "When hard times come about and things we don't understand happen here on earth, through scripture, He promises to be God and transform bad or evil into positive and use it to the benefit of our good, only through Christ!" It says in Romans 8:28, "And we know that God causes everything to work together for the good of those who love God and are called according to his purpose for them."

Even though adversity can be hard and is hard at times, don't allow Satan to bog you down with guilt or create an unworthy feeling through those circumstances in you. Let God take control of those bad circumstances and allow Him to use those bad experiences, which can be transformed to your benefit where only God receives the glory. He will walk beside you every step of the way, in and through situations where you may feel, "I can't go on any longer!" With that said, you are correct; you, yourself, cannot go on any longer doing it on your own, but with Christ living in and through you and doing a good work, He will prevail and use the bad and evil to work for your benefit, which is where He will receive the glory.

During any of the referenced circumstances, I didn't have answers for anyone, even for my myself, as I knew I had to trust God. I'm not sure that was always or ever the answer I gave them when I was inquired, "What are you going to do?" But I knew in my heart I just needed to trust Him. I'm still, to this day, asked, "What are you going to do?" When I'm faced with a decision, whether it be small or big, I'm going to do the same thing I've been shown by the Lord, which is to trust and surrender to Him. Now that you are close to the end of this book, I hope you see that only trusting the Lord is the only method that works. We, ourselves, and those around us desperately want to know the future, even tomorrow, but it takes pressures off us when we just wake up each day and live for Him, allowing Him to be in the driver's seat while we act as the passenger. We all have goals, dreams, and passions, which we should, but we shouldn't be directing our lives on our own without prayer, counsel, and guidance from the Lord as He knows you from the inside out, better than you know yourself.

Often, people won't ever understand how or why you make the decisions you make, but when God is leading you or has led you to a place you know He wants or wanted you to go, then an explanation won't be easy to anyone, especially if they don't understand or approve of your decision(s). I've found that the closer you become to the Lord, more of those around you won't understand your decisions or why you do the things you do. While God isn't a God that we understand ourselves, therefore, when He asks something of you, it's only Him that could do such things that He has laid on your heart. Let God be God, and next time someone asks, "What are you going to do," reply with, "I'm going to trust the Lord" "Follow through with obedience and watch God be God," which not anyone will understand nor comprehend, but know He will receive the glory in and through you if you follow through with obedience!

CHAPTER 25

ETERNAL DESTINATION

A s I bring this journey to a conclusion, I've been on multiple trips lately with multiple people. No matter where the trip was, how long it was, or how much fun we had, I always found myself stating, "I can't wait to be home!" It's always fun to travel and experience the things He has allowed us to experience while living on this earth however long we're allowed, but we're meant for an eternal home. I find it interesting how, on vacations or trips, we're always wanting to be back to our earthly home, but why don't we long for our eternal home? I believe that we are supposed to enjoy our time while here on this earth and do all we can to honor the Lord and show others His love so that they can experience that as well, but we are wired for our final destination.

Our destination when we leave this earth depends on that ONE decision that you make. God has already done His part sending His one and only Son to die on a cross for you so that you can have a relationship here on earth with Him and then spend eternity with the ONE that you are wired for; which is to worship and give all the glory to. He has created you with purpose, a mind, a heart, and wired you with compassion, joy, laughter, and so many other incredible things that are meant for His glory and purpose. Just because you attempt to live the Christian life doesn't mean you'll have a trouble-free life, which you already know by reading this book, but what it does mean that through addictions, bad relationships, pornography, debt, divorce, hurt, feeling lost, and feeling I can't go on any longer like this the answer is that "You don't have to, and God doesn't want you to!"

Once you accept Christ into your heart (I'll lead you through that prayer further down in just a bit), and you know He has purpose for your life, you know He can remove you from those hurts and pains through bad life choices. You know He can remove debt through surrender, you know He can repair a marriage, you know He can take away that addiction that you felt you could never get away from. Christ will restore your life and make you new again. Once you accept Him into your life and decide you want to follow His ways, it's called being "born again." No, you're not being born again physically, but spiritually, you're made new, and your sins are remembered no more as those chains have already been broken when He died for you. It's just a simple decision and the best and most important decision you'll ever make throughout your entire life, and it goes like this:

> Father, I know I'm a sinner. I've lived in ways I know were not pleasing to You and have lived selfishly and haven't been living for You. I believe You sent Your one and only Son to this earth and lived a perfect life and that He was crucified and shed His blood on a cross to forgive me. I now ask that You'll come into my heart, forgive me of my sins, and make me the person You want me to be and change my life forever.

If you just prayed that prayer and meant it in your heart, you will now spend eternity with Jesus. Now just because you prayed that prayer doesn't mean your life will be all happiness and riches, but it does mean that you'll now spend forever with your Creator, and through those troubled times which are going to happen, Christ will be there with you to walk alongside of you through those, until you reach your eternal home. And now because of those few seconds it took for you to say that prayer, your eternal home will now be spent forever with Jesus. I encourage you to first start a daily reading plan where you will grow in His Word. It doesn't have to be six chapters a day or even one chapter a day, but reading His Word will change your thoughts and your actions through the way you live your life. Next, I challenge you to get plugged in a local church, or find some way to be involved with other believers around you. The Christian life is hard, in fact, it's impossible, as only Christ conquered it, which is why we need those solid believers around us challenging us daily to walk in His ways. It might be hard, but *once you wholeheartedly give your life to the Lord, you'll never look back because it was worth His life to die for you*! As we long to get home after those road trips and vacations, you can now long for and live for your eternal home, and that's heaven!!

> This means that anyone who belongs to Christ has become a new person. The old life is gone; a new life has begun! (2 Cor. 5:17)

Insert your name in this blank, and now say, "I, _____,
will spend eternity with Christ and will live a life pleasing and desperate for Him. Thank you, Lord, for accepting me the way I am and change me to who you want me to become and use me for your glory!!

ISN'T THAT INCREDIBLE!

CONCLUSION

I've been more transparent throughout this reading than I've ever been with anyone on this earth as only God knows my heart. There isn't anyone, until now, that knows of my situation between my parents throughout my childhood as far as church and tithing and how I truly felt through the time of their divorce. Not anyone, including James K. and Josh, had knowledge of what I sacrificed to be able to do what all I did for them, and not always because I wanted to but was called to through sacred concern. No family, friends, or anyone had the insight about my financial situation, from credit card debt to personal loans and student loans. It's not been easy to share any of these things, realizing as this gets published and that anyone who reads "Intimately Acquainted" will now know a substantial amount about me, but that's what's intended as I hope it encourages you to surrender to the Lord not just parts of your life but your WHOLE life, and YES...including your finances!

I do not share any of this to brag about what the Lord has brought me to nor brought me through. Each of our lives are completely different, and you may have a different sacred concern or a different longing on your heart to change a life in a completely different way. You may have that burden on you to feed the hungry, travel across seas and do missions. You may have a heart to help disabled children. You might even feel led to adopt a child from China and bring him or her into your family. Whatever your calling or sacred concern, never fail to ignore it. Throughout the calling or situation, the Lord is leading you to do something, and there won't be anything like it, even though it's costing you something. It might cost you a financial strain, it might cost you a job, a move, a friend, or maybe even your life, but I can promise you one thing, if the Lord has called you to it, He will get you through it. It won't be easy, but anything is possible when you have the Creator of the universe living inside of you, guiding and directing you and helping you each day to make decisions to go in His path.

My heartbeat and desire for this book was to share some of my struggles and triumphs and revealing those in complete transparency to you. Just because you hit a roadblock or what you might think is a dead end in life, know that with God, there are no dead ends—it's just a redirection, and He will always get you through as long as you lean not on your own understanding but on His. When you focus your efforts more so to help others prosper, somehow, your attitude of gratitude is filled, more so than if the focus was on yourself. This doesn't line up with what the world tells you, but when you live knowing the earth is temporary, it will give you an eternal satisfaction. Christ is ultimately the one to show and lead the way and will forever show you *ways to make a way,* if you'll trust the *Waymaker and become intimately acquainted with Christ*!" I love you and know *God has purpose for your life*!

CITING PAGE

I. *Today God Is First*, devotional by Os Hillman, iDisciple.org (Introduction)

If we desire to fully walk with Christ, there is a cost. We may give intellectual assent and go along with His principles and do fine; however, if we are fully given over to Him and His will for our life, it will be a life that will have adversity. The Bible is clear that humans do not achieve greatness without having their sinful will broken.

If God has plans to greatly use you in the lives of others, you can expect your trials to be even greater than those of others. Why? Because, like Joseph who went through greater trials than most patriarchs, your calling may have such responsibility that God cannot afford to entrust it to you without ensuring your complete faithfulness to the call. He has much invested in you on behalf of others. He may want to speak through your life to a greater degree than through another. The events of your life would become the frame for the message He wants to speak through you.

Do not fear the path that God may lead you on. Embrace it. For God may bring you down a path in your life to ensure the reward of your inheritance. "For our light and momentary troubles are achieving for us an eternal glory that far outweighs them all" (2 Corinthians 4:17). (Os Hillman)

II. Francis Chan, *Crazy Love*, Twitter

If you wait until all of your own issues are gone before helping others, it will never happen. This is a trap that millions have fallen into, not realizing that our own sanctification happens as we minister to others. (Francis Chan, *Crazy Love*, page ——)

III. Francis Chan, *Crazy Love*, Twitter

The truth is that the Spirit of the living God is guaranteed to ask you to go somewhere or do something you wouldn't normally want or choose to do. (Francis Chan, *Crazy Love*, page ——)

IV. November 23, 2014, "Sacred Concern" quote, Hillside Christian Church, Series: "Goldilocks," Sermon Title: "The Other Extreme," Speaker: Tommy Politz, page ——

V. March 9, 2013. "When God Says Wait" quotes. All quotes came from the same sermon message. Trinity Fellowship, Lubbock, Texas. Sermon Title: "When God Says Wait," John Spurling, pages ——; pages ——

ABOUT THE AUTHOR

Jeff Fiedler was born on November 1979. He grew up in a small town of Hobbs, New Mexico, and now resides in Amarillo, Texas. He graduated from Hobbs High School and then went on to further his education in Texas at Amarillo College with a drafting degree. He then went on to West Texas A&M University where he majored in business management and obtained a bachelor's degree. Jeff is now an owner of The Drawing Board, a successful drafting and design company which creates custom home plans throughout the Texas Panhandle. While Jeff works full time at The Drawing Board, he also works part-time for the 911 communications center. Jeff attends Hillside Christian Church and has previously worked as a youth pastor in Amarillo. Jeff has had prior experience in professional motorsports while touring the drag racing circuit across the United States. During his spare time, he remains interested in drag racing while doing other things such as playing drums, playing golf and tennis, traveling, mountain biking, and riding his dirt bike with friends when time allows. Jeff enjoys spending time with friends and family and is passionate about mentoring high school and college-age students. Throughout the daily demands of life, Jeff creates time to write and encourage others with what God has laid on his heart through speaking engagements, text, and social media.